keep the fire!

Approaching your senior
years with perspective
and passion

DON ANDERSON
FOREWORD BY DR. HOWARD HENDRICKS

MULTNOMAH BOOKS

KEEP THE FIRE!

© 1994 by Donald E. Anderson

published by Multnomah Books
a part of the Questar publishing family

International Standard Book Number: 0-88070-653-8

Printed in the United States of America

The author wishes to acknowledge the editorial assistance of Jane Rodgers.

Cover photo: Allsport/Vandystadt

For information:
Questar Publishers, Inc.
Post Office Box 1720
Sisters, Oregon 97759

94 95 96 97 98 99 00 01 02 03 — 10 9 8 7 6 5 4 3 2 1

To my Pearl of great price.
Your excellence and faithful encouragement
make me aware of two things:
I married over my head. And I married a saint.
We've come a long way, baby, but we ain't home yet!

CONTENTS

FOREWORD

The Western world teems with older individuals treated more as liabilities than assets. Even churches have joined with society in sidelining seniors and trivializing their contributions and needs. Only those individuals whose years have produced significant prestige and material assets remain on the active roll call of honorees. Thus, Don Anderson's *Keep the Fire!* is a timely reminder.

Rooted in a scriptural base, these chapters teach afresh how to make maturity mean what God intended. What is the purpose of growing up, of developing perspective, of living a life? And how should younger people feel about and respond to the thundering approach of later years? Anderson answers these and other critical questions from a positive perspective, challenging the concept that we should slow down as the race wears on and, instead, urging us to go for the gold.

"How Old Is Old?" What's involved in "Planning for Graduation"? And how can a fast-paced, independently minded American ever hope to master the art of "Learning to Lean"? These chapters alone are worth the investment of time and shelf space.

Jeanne and I find ourselves in that company labeled "over the hill." We confront these issues not only personally but with our peers who more and more are seeking guidelines for this complex stage of life. Few have been more helpful to so many over the years than Don Anderson as he has translated the Bible into practical rules for living. Once again, with heart and a head of solid advice, he has hit the mark.

Keep the Fire! kindles a radiance that reveals the true value of piling up birthdays. Unlike candles on a cake this flame lights the inner spirit of the elder laureate with eternal hope.

HOWARD G. HENDRICKS
Distinguished Professor
Chairman, Center for Christian Leadership
Dallas Theological Seminary

PREFACE

America is graying...literally. The first wave of baby boomers has already crashed upon the shores of mid-life. Their parents, a generation beyond that milestone, are senior adults. With advances in health care and medicine, people are living longer. Senior adulthood, and consequently, retirement, can last a long, long time. The challenge for the committed Christian is to redeem that time.

Picture yourself driving down the freeway on a beautiful winter day. The old Suburban has 80,000 miles on it, but it's humming along on cruise control like it always has since leaving the showroom floor. All of a sudden you start hearing strange noises. Could it be your imagination? No. The noises are getting louder. A couple of trouble lights on the dash tell you to check the engine.

For many, that's just the way it happens with aging. A sharp pain, a pulled muscle, a ruptured disk...and maintenance on the equipment begins. We begin the wonderful season of our lives when we play hurt. We find we must learn to play through the pain.

The challenge for believers is to lay it on, not to let up, in the last, most crucial quarter: "So then, banish anxiety from your heart and cast off the troubles of your body, for youth and vigor are meaningless" (Ecclesiastes 11:10 NIV).

Retirement for the believer should be far more than a wholesale pursuit of leisure and comfort. Society tells us we've earned a rest. We deserve to enjoy ourselves. We ought to indulge, kick back, take things easy, be content with golf, gardening, travel, and recreational vehicles. What an appalling waste of time, intelligence, and abilities! R & R is fine, but not as a lifestyle.

Sixty-five needn't signal the end of significant activity and productivity in our lives. The work of Jesus Christ knows no age limits or cultural boundaries. There is always more than enough to be done and too few to do it.

Paul's letter to the Philippians provides solutions and encouragement for the final laps of life. Not specifically addressed to seniors, the epistle is still a gold mine of guidance for that phase of life. Whenever we appropriately apply Scripture to life, we can have the quiet confidence that God's promise is trustworthy: "So is my word that goes out from my mouth: It will not return to me empty, but will accomplish what I desire and achieve the purpose for which I sent it" (Isaiah 55:11 NIV).

The time to plan for a godly senior life is long before you get there. As my fortyish friend Connie said when we were discussing this book: "I can't wait to get a copy so I'll understand what my parents are going through. Actually, I guess I need to read it myself so I'll be ready!" She was right. You must prepare for the biggest game of your life before the final innings.

American culture tells seniors they are over the hill. Wrong! We're only on a roll. Let's keep the fire!

SPECIAL THANKS

Just as "no man is an island," no book is the product of a single hand. Many deserve heartfelt thanks, including these folks:

The congregations of Hide-A-Way Lake and Emerald Bay community churches for fifteen years of friendship and support. What a joy it is to see you keeping the fire!

The godly professors from Talbot School of Theology who are my valued mentors: Vernon Grounds, Norman Wakefield, Grant Howard, Richard Mohline, Robert Coleman, Charles Sell, Gary McIntosh, Boyd Luter.

Dr. Larry Covin for developing and administering the senior adult survey.

John Van Diest, for recommending an old friend to a top-notch outfit. Thanks, Johnny!

The team at Questar, including Dan Rich, David Carlson, and Michele Tennesen. What a delight it is to work with such committed professionals.

Becky Durost Fish and Carol Bartley—special kudos for their editorial expertise.

The board of directors of Don Anderson Ministries—friends all. You have encouraged this project and my writing pursuits from the start. Great is your faithfulness!

Jan Terry, Sandra Mitcham, Jean Powell, and Genevieve Martin of the Ministries staff. No one can measure the value of your contribution to this book and our work as a whole. You are truly God's gifts to us.

Jane Rodgers, whose name literally means "gift of God," and describes her well, too. Thanks for helping an old marathoner pull it all together on the written page.

Last but not least, my sweetheart Pearl and our own Fab Five, their mates, and the seven (so far) perfect grandchildren made in heaven. Thanks for your love and patience as Grandpa grows up.

CHAPTER 1

HOW OLD IS OLD... AND WHAT'S IT TO YOU?

You are as young as you feel after trying to prove it.

LOU ERICKSON

I just passed sixty on a dead run. Wow! I'm growing up fast. And I'm having the time of my life! I'm excited about the new things I'm experiencing and learning. But some things I've discovered need to be changed.

We should drop the term *old age*. It conjures up images of bedpans, dentures, and nursing homes. Old age comes just before senility, people tell me. Not that senility is anything to worry about. We won't know when it hits us. It may even be kind of nice, meeting new people every day—again and again and again.

> Elderly widow to widower: Someone asked me to marry him last night and I can't remember who it was.
>
> Widower: That's funny. I asked someone to marry me last night, and I can't remember who it was either![1]

Aging *can* work to our advantage. "Yes, you get to hide your own Easter eggs," quipped retiree Olive.

Dame Agatha Christie reaped unusual dividends in the twilight years of her marriage to Dr. H. E. Mallowan. Said the renowned mystery writer of her archaeologist husband, "The older I get, the more interested he becomes in me."[2]

What does old age mean to you? Social Security? Sunbelt condos? RVs? Golf? Fishing? Travel? Freedom? Leisure?

Whatever the words mean to you, come along with me. The best is yet to be.

USE IT OR LOSE IT

Growing old never crossed my mind when I was in my twenties and thirties. But after fifteen years pastoring two churches with large populations of senior adults, my attention has been sharply focused on life after sixty.

As I passed middle age, an arthritic hip aggravated from years of running marathons teamed up with a bad Achilles tendon to nearly cripple me. After hip replacement surgery, I now spend hours beating up on my stationary bike. Lately I'm looking forward to comparing notes in heaven with the patriarch Jacob. His bum hip (wrestling injury) caused him to lean on his staff till the end of his days (Hebrews 11:21). We should have a lot in common.

I know what it is to see the body start to deteriorate with time. There are days I get up and feel like I need a grease job and an oil change before I can get back on track. Joints are stiff; muscles ache; my brain tells me my body is threatening a walk-out—or a sit-down. A hip and a knee are already on strike, and the rest of the members take longer every morning to give me the green light.

The truth is I'm wearing out, and there are no guarantees on this hunk of flesh, blood, and bone I call home. Old age is uncomfortably close. The season of retirement is just around the bend.

My prayer at this point is for my attitude to be as positive as the apostle Paul's in 2 Corinthians 4:16: "Therefore we do not lose heart, but though our outer man is decaying, yet our inner man is being renewed day by day."

The hills and curves of the last half of life are ahead. It's okay to slow down to maneuver safely, but I can't take my foot off the throttle.

The people who age best and last longest are those who stay at it. If we're planning to be put out to pasture, chances are that pretty soon we'll be going to seed, too. We use it or lose it. And sometimes we lose it anyway, so may God help us laugh a lot and live a lot. I don't want to grow bitter. Like our dear friend Ernest Burch, I hope I can roar with laughter when the oph-thalmologist tells me, "You can see more than you can catch."

Maturity milestones may signal the end to many things, including a way of life as comfortable as a favorite pair of run-ning shoes. But our latter years can also be our best yet, as we see from these encouraging verses of Scripture:

For through me your days will be many,
    and years will be added to your life (Proverbs 9:11 NIV).

The Lord blessed the latter part of Job's life more than
    the first.... And so he died, old and full of years
                                (Job 42:12,17 NIV).

17

> The righteous will flourish like a palm tree,
> > they will grow like a cedar of Lebanon....
> *They will still bear fruit in old age,*
> > they will stay fresh and green (Psalm 92:12,14 NIV,
> > > > > > > > > > italics mine).

HOW OLD IS OLD?

The legendary baseball player Satchel Paige once posed the question, "How old would you be if you didn't know how old you are?"[3] His words illustrate an opinion psychologists and gerontologists have long concluded to be true: Old age is essentially a matter of the mind.

Yes, physical infirmities may slow us down considerably as we reach our sixties, seventies, and eighties. But we won't really be old until we feel old. As doctors Minirth, Meier, and Reed put it, "Individuals can be elderly at age fifty, or they can be young at age ninety."[4] According to Bill and Lillian Mason, "The thermostat of true aging is set by one's mind, by serenity of spirit, by continued growth, and by purposeful activity."[5]

General Douglas MacArthur kept an essay on his office wall which contained these reflections on staying young: "Youth is not a time of life, it is a state of mind. You are as young as your faith, as old as your doubts, as young as your self-confidence, as old as your fear, as young as your hope, as old as your despair."[6]

If old age is primarily a matter of the mind, what about the body? The fact is, old age isn't physically what it used to be. In 1900, the average life expectancy for American males was forty-six years; for females, forty-eight. Today, the average life expectancy at birth has increased to seventy years for men and seventy-eight for women. At the turn of the century, fewer than a million Americans had reached their seventy-fifth birthdays. Now nine million individuals, one-fourth of the older adult population, have achieved or passed that birthday milestone.[7] Social scientists predict that the trend toward longevity will continue. Leland F. Cooley and Lee M. Cooley write in *How To Avoid the Retirement Trap*:

> Gerontological research going on in the nation's leading medical schools and in foundation laboratories promises still more dramatic extensions of the life cycle. And geneticists, standing on the threshold of discoveries that many find frightening and "ungodly," foresee a day not too distant when they will be able to "blueprint" a super race—extend a person's useful years to a full century and an average life expectancy to 125 years or more.[8]

Americans aged sixty-five and above numbered 28,530,000 according to the Census Bureau's mid eighties update. That figure swelled to over 31,000,000 in 1990. Even the "oldest of the old" are increasing in number. The second-fastest growing age group in the United States consists of men and women aged eighty-five and above.[9] The Census Bureau reports that by the year 2000, four-generation families will be the norm. And by 2030, the entire baby boom generation—one third of the present U.S. population—will be senior citizens. That's seventy-seven million people![10]

The significance of all this? Americans are living longer and staying healthier longer. Older Americans are comprising an increasing percentage of the population as the "graying of

America" becomes an undeniable reality. This gray revolution will impact our social institutions and churches in ways we are only starting to imagine.

AGING: A BIBLICAL LOOK

In the plan of God, aging is inevitable. Scripture shows us that a long life is often (not always) a blessing from the Lord, a reward of righteousness. Abraham lived to the age of 175, Isaac to 180, Jacob to 147, Moses to 120 (see Genesis 25:7, 35:28, 47:28; Deuteronomy 34:7).

Two New Testament characters illustrate the beauty of lengthy and righteous lives. These seniors, Simeon and Anna, must have been a blessing to all who met them.

Simeon lived in Jerusalem. We read of him in Luke 2:25-32, as he responds to the Holy Spirit's leading and goes to the temple one day, just in time to meet Mary, Joseph, and their newborn baby boy.

Jesus' parents had likely left their quarters in Bethlehem early that morning. It pleased the new mother to get out in public after a month of seclusion. They arrived in Jerusalem as the Middle Eastern sun grew warm. Feeling a bit like two mice in the palace, the little family walked inside the temple's outer gate. Joseph carried the pigeons; Mary cradled her precious treasure, Jesus.

The surreal quality of the day was confirmed from the lips of an old gentleman they didn't know, a man who took their baby in his arms. What an imposing sight Simeon must have been: white hair flowing, beard glistening in the sun, head bowed, shoulders stooped with age as he cradled at his breast, God in human flesh. The Shekinah glory had come back to the temple. With gratitude and awe Simeon announced: "Now Lord, Thou dost let Thy bond-servant depart, in peace, according to Thy word; for mine eyes have seen Thy salvation, which Thou hast prepared in the presence of all peoples, a light of revelation to the Gentiles, and the glory of Thy people Israel" (Luke 2:29-32).

Scripture says Simeon was "righteous" and "devout," and that the "Holy Spirit was upon him" (Luke 2:25). No doubt Simeon spent many nights on his knees, praying for God to send his nation's last best hope, her only consolation, Messiah. God knew Simeon's faithfulness. God saw his heart. And God promised Simeon that he would not die before he had seen the Chosen One (Luke 2:26).

In Luke 2 we have the picture of a godly man, full of years, whom the Lord remembered. Holding and blessing baby Jesus, Simeon was content. More than content, he was ready to go out in a blaze of glory. No regrets. No second guesses. Simeon was one satisfied senior—awake, alive, and available to God in his old age.

Another elderly servant of God saw the Savior in the temple that day. Her name was Anna, a prophetess of the tribe of Asher. When we meet her in Scripture, she is eighty-four years young. Widowed only seven years into her marriage, Anna's cup had overflowed with heartache and grief. She could have become angry at God, as so many do who suffer great loss. Instead, Anna fled to God.

As a young widow, Anna dedicated herself to serving God in the temple. For perhaps as many as sixty years, she busied herself about God's work. She learned that the Father never causes His children needless tears, that broken hearts are meant to be built upon, that senior adulthood can be lived out fruitfully, graciously, and vigorously.

As far as we know, Anna never retired. Much of her work as a prophetess involved prayer and fasting in the temple. She never left the place!

Spying Jesus in Simeon's arms, Anna told everyone in the temple that day about the Holy One now in their midst (Luke 2:39). The climax of her life finds her praising and spreading news about Jesus—a perfect pattern to follow. No matter how old we are, like Anna, we can concentrate on Christ and be consumed with accomplishing His purposes and plans.

Not all people in the Bible managed to live out their senior years as unselfishly and productively as Simeon and Anna. Noah got drunk and did nothing substantial for the last 350 years of his life. Eli failed as a father and priest and died fat, old, and inactive. Solomon left a thousand widows and a divided kingdom. In his final years even good King Asa looked to guidance from other kings and doctors instead of God.

But for every Solomon or Eli in Scripture, there is a Simeon, an Anna, a precious saint who ran the race well without stopping short.

A godly senior adulthood is useful and exemplary. It models life to watching generations. It doesn't quit, take a siesta, or pause for an extended breather before physical death. To the very end, it is lived creatively, unselfishly, faithfully, and passionately, with definite goals in view.

NOT AN END, A BEGINNING

Many people don't respond to the inevitable losses of aging with good will, humor, or hope. Reduced physical abilities anger them. A spouse's illness or death sparks resentment. Hurts run deep as friends die or move away. Hypersensitivity replaces sweetness of spirit.

The adjectives cantankerous, crabby, grouchy, and grumpy now describe Gramps and Gram. Sullen, scolding, selfish, and just flat scared, we might add. Age has rained on their parade, interfering with life as they are used to living it. The biggest ego-buster of them all? They are losing control. They are going out like they came in: dependent. And they are mad at the world for the mess they are in.

But it doesn't have to be that way.

Simeon and Anna defied senior stereotypes. They lived life full throttle, still sensitive, serving, and seeking. They saw life and lived it positively.

This isn't to say growing old is easy. There are no guarantees that we'll stay healthy, pain-free, financially comfortable, or mentally alert up to the end. We will experience losing, leaving, and letting go—what author Judith Viorst calls life's "necessary losses." Yet we can still view the mile markers of senior adulthood not as an end, but as a fabulous beginning.

A booster rocket to launch us into the next exciting phase of our journey is to realize, like Simeon and Anna, that advanced age does not necessarily signal the end of significant production. Surely Ronald Reagan, who spent the bulk of his seventies as president of the United States, would agree with that. So would countless others.

Consider what these individuals accomplished while in their eighties: Albert Schweitzer headed a hospital in Africa; Michelangelo designed the church of Santa Maria degli Angeli; Winston Churchill wrote his four-volume *A History of the*

English-Speaking Peoples; Ben Franklin engineered the compromise that led to the ratification of the Constitution.[11]

Neither should we forget that Grandma Moses painted her first picture at seventy-six; Colonel Sanders made his first million in his seventies; Amos Alonzo Stagg didn't retire from collegiate coaching till age ninety-six; and George Adamson of *Born Free* fame ran his primitive wildlife camp in eastern Kenya right up to the day of his tragic (and yes, untimely) death by homicide at age eighty-three.

In the 1990s, Mother Theresa finally shows a few health-related signs of slowing down. Former President Richard Nixon, as an octogenarian, acted as an unofficial ambassador to Moscow. Bob Hope still entertains the troops. Actress Jessica Tandy garners one Academy Award nomination after another. Movie star Jack Palance even wins his first Oscar and celebrates by doing one-armed push-ups on stage. George Burns plans his one hundredth birthday for Carnegie Hall.

As long as you are alive, why not really live?

SEEING THE POSITIVE

A centenarian interviewed the other day was asked what she liked best about being over one hundred. "Why, the loss of peer pressure," she replied. That is seeing the positive.

Senior adulthood is an era of production potential. Seeing the possibilities should give us an attitude boost. Another lift comes as we realize that senior life is temporary. It's the decisive lap in the grand race of life. Let's make the most of what we have while we have it.

In John Quincy Adams's final years, he walked slowly and feebly down a Boston street one day. A longtime friend stopped and shook the former president's hand, asking, "And how is John Quincy Adams today?"

"Thank you," replied the elder statesman. "John Quincy Adams is well, quite well, I thank you. But the house in which he lives at present is becoming quite dilapidated. It is tottering upon its foundations. Time and the seasons have nearly destroyed it. Its roof is pretty well worn out. Its walls are much shattered, and it trembles with every wind. The old tenement is becoming almost uninhabitable, and I think John Quincy Adams will have to move out of it soon. But he himself is quite well, quite well."[12]

What a beautiful perspective! Someday we'll run out of years—but that, too, will be great. In the words of the apostle Paul: "For we know that if the earthly tent which is our house is torn down, we have a building from God, a house not made with hands, eternal in the heavens. For indeed in this house we groan, longing to be clothed with our dwelling from heaven" (2 Corinthians 5:1-2).

I recommend taping this passage to your mirror as your first silver threads appear among the gold and your wrinkles marry and give birth to triplets. What a lift! It's not what you are losing, but what you have left which counts. It's not where you have been, but where you are going which brings joy, unspeakable and full of glory.

Since this is so, I recommend we put problems behind us. Let's focus on our assets as we mature. Let's determine, right now, to see the positive. Forgetting what lies behind, let's press on to what is in front. The way we run the final laps determines how well we finish. Isaiah 46:4 gives us encouragement from God for rounding the final curve: "Even to your old age and gray hairs I am he, I am he who will sustain you. I have made you and I will carry you; I will sustain you and I will rescue you" (NIV).

DON'T STOP TILL YOU DROP

"Shop till you drop," reads one of my wife's favorite bumper stickers. Pearl would be content to die trying to find *it* at the mall, whatever *it* is. The attitude conveyed by that message also applies to growing older: It is good to persevere toward a goal until we are totally spent. Maybe we need a senior adult bumper sticker that reads, "Don't stop till you drop." Or maybe, "Live it up till they lay you down." How about, "Keep the spark till you park"?

Whether or not we formally shift gears from a career as we mature, there is a whole lot of life from which we never quit. Many aspects of human existence do not change when we stop punching a clock. These areas are non-negotiable—without compromise—for the Christian. Let's look at seven parts of life which should not stop till we do.

1. Marriage. The divine desire for a marriage relationship is till death do us part. Jesus says of the sanctity of marriage, "Consequently they are no more two, but one flesh. What therefore God has joined together, let no man separate" (Matthew 19:6, see also 19:4-5).

When a man and woman say, "I do," it is supposed to be a done deal. They have started something that they must finish. The consequences are devastating if either partner stops working on the relationship. Yet so often this is what happens. We settle for less. Somewhere between wedding night perfume and mid-life morning breath, one of the love birds flies the coop. We opt out when God has clearly said, "Stay in."

The thrill of going for the gold and achieving at least fifty years of married life together should be the aim of every couple marching down the aisle. If I had my way, it would be written in the contract. My wife and I are challenged and inspired by the many gold medal "marriagists" we know who have made it together fifty anniversaries or more.

Pearl and I have now lasted through forty years of marriage, five kids, seven pets, the mid-life crisis, the empty-nest syndrome, and a ton of funny and unforgettable experiences. We're glad to be Grandma and Gramps for a slew of young ones. Two granddaughters even share the middle name Pearl. With my own sweetheart we're getting a regular string.

We're finding intimacy really begins when the last kid gets married and the last pet dies. I know the rest of life won't be a downhill slide. It never is. But I am sure glad my Pearl will be along for the ride. We are having so much fun aging together. She is a treasure! I don't know what I would do without her.

2. *Spiritual growth.* Spiritual growth should likewise never stop. Keep your eyes on the prize. Press on toward the goal. You are in a spiritual war all the way home. The world, the flesh, and the devil are setting out land mines everywhere, and they'd like to take you out of God's Word and away from His fellowship. Refuse to pull over and park. Stay in the race. In marathons, the meat wagon always passes by to pick up those who want to quit. Don't get on. Realize you can grow spiritually till the day you leave this world for the next.

I wish you could have met Hazel Fels. Hers was the only funeral sermon I ever preached which had been written by the deceased. She didn't dictate on her deathbed. But when it came time to honor the memory of this godly woman, all I had to do was pick up her well-worn Bible and speak on the passages she had underlined again and again. I used her own notes and comments, some penned only a few days before her final illness. She never quit growing spiritually.

A friend says she starts off slow at most things, then tapers off. May that never describe our Christian growth!

3. *Intellectual development.* The slogan of the United Negro College Fund, "A mind is a terrible thing to waste," may be accurately applied to seniors as well. The mind of any person—young or old—is much too wonderful to waste. Sometimes senile dementias such as Alzheimer's disease severely impair mental processes. But quite often senior citizens are mentally alive and well, yet grossly inactive. Dale Evans Rogers, no slouch herself, quotes septuagenarian Dr. Jonas Salk:

> At one time, our biggest problems concerned diseases like poliomyelitis. Now we are becoming aware of another type of problem, the acute disorders of minds facing uselessness, highly developed minds suddenly without use or purpose.
>
> However, this doesn't have to be a problem of old age if people continue to grow as human beings and make life meaningful whether they are employed or not....
>
> Without a constructive purpose life becomes destructive.[13]

It doesn't have to be. First Peter 1:13 is far from a call to use-lessness and complacency: "Therefore, gird your minds for action, keep sober in spirit, fix your hope completely on the grace to be brought to you at the revelation of Jesus Christ." Get focused and feed on God's Word. Read a book a week. Memorize Scripture. You can do it!

4. Physical exercise. Eighty-year-old Walter Stack runs marathons in the Bay Area. When asked by an interviewer after a daily run what he would do when it got so cold outside that his teeth would chatter, Walter Stack replied, "I'd leave them in my locker."

Whether or not you run marathons, physical fitness should be an aim at all stages of life. Some seniors choose golf, tennis, power-walking, aerobics, cross-country skiing, or stationary bicycling. Staying as physically in shape as possible enables us to more effectively serve God. Our energy levels remain high; we master our bodies (mostly). Some of the old parts may fall off while we're working out, but that's just the price we pay.

The apostle Paul understood the principle that physical toughness helps produce a disciplined spiritual life: "But I buffet my body and make it my slave, lest possibly, after I have preached to others, I myself should be disqualified" (1 Corinthians 9:27).

General Chuck Yeager writes of his own determination to stay active:

Life is as unpredictable as flying in combat. If the day comes when a flight surgeon tells me I can't fly anymore in high performance jets, I can always sneak out back and fly ultra-lights. Just like when the day dawns that Andy and I can't manage our treks into the Sierra to fish for golden trout...there are still nearby lakes and plenty of rowboats. You do what you can for as long as you can, and when you finally can't, you do the next best thing. You back up but you don't give up.[14]

5. *Goals for the future.* New York state senator Thomas C. Desmond once said, "Keep thinking of things to be done tomorrow rather than what you did yesterday. Many experts suggest that we should have goals for our senior years. We should retire to something. A concerted effort toward even an apparently modest goal can help prevent premature shutdown."[15]

People cease to enjoy life when they no longer have a reason to get up in the morning. We desperately need goals in the golden years.

The idea that she could still set goals brought a glow to the face of a sixty-five-year-old missionary I recently counseled. She had come home from the field for the last time and thought she was washed up. No way! As we'll see, the apostle Paul gives at least ten godly goals in the pages of Philippians for living life fully to the finish.

6. *Having new experiences.* While we never stop having new experiences, we often fail to recognize or acknowledge them. May we never lose our wonder and excitement over exploring and enjoying new things. Too many of us live too short and die too long.

Traveling to new places, meeting new people, doing new things, all make the final phase of life most fulfilling. Seniors Tom and Olive have snowmobiled in a Montana wilderness, climbed Indian ruins in Guatemala, snorkeled in the Fiji Islands, and gone mud fishing in the Gulf of Mexico.

Stop ruling out so many possibilities! Don't be afraid of the unknown! Don't be afraid to keep climbing, "Forgetting what lies behind and reaching forward to what lies ahead" (Philippians 3:13). You can do it, and you'll be glad you did.

7. *Serving others.* Jesus reminded us of the importance of serving others: "It is not so among you, but whoever wishes to become great among you shall be your servant, and whoever wishes to be first among you shall be your slave; just as the Son of Man did not come to be served, but to serve, and to give His life a ransom for many" (Matthew 20:26-28).

Me-firstness permeates our society. In the gray years, me-firstness means spending time doing what we want to do for our own personal benefit. You can almost hear the chorus: "You've earned it. You've done your share. Now do your own thing! Have fun! Relax. Slip into neutral. Hit the hot tub!"

A certain amount of leisure is fine. I enjoy travel, fun times, and occasional seclusion. But I've never found a place in Scripture that excuses us from serving. Instead, we are instructed by the apostle Paul to "bear one another's burdens, and thus fulfill the law of Christ" (Galatians 6:2).

Me-firstness thinks only of the moment, the pleasure, the temporal. It doesn't concern itself with the eternal.

In a recent *Rolling Stone* magazine survey, forty percent of baby boomers surveyed said that there would be no conditions under which they would be willing to fight for their country.[16] Only one in three boomers regularly votes.[17] That's scary. How desperately the generations coming up need examples of older men and women unafraid to serve, sacrifice, and participate.

Jesus never stopped giving. Only hours before He went to Calvary, He exhausted Himself answering His followers' questions and washing their feet. His death was the ultimate sacrificial service for us all.

When we actively participate in the lives of others, we have little time to feel sorry for ourselves or to become consumed with our concerns. We are freed from the shackles of selfishness. Older people who refuse to let up and instead choose to "live it up" with direction and intensity are examples the Pepsi generation needs to see.

Blasting Off—Not Fizzling Out

We need to view senior adulthood as more than an opportunity for maximum leisure and minimal service. God has assignments for us at sixty-five, seventy, eighty—just as He did at twenty-two.

Getting up in years brings challenges, but despite the difficulties, every day can be an intensely positive experience. It is essential for us to adopt positive mental attitudes. As senior adults that means we:

1. Determine not to let events bother us.
2. Learn to let go when it is time to let go.
3. Recognize that it is often necessary to dig a little deeper and just keep going, taking our licks and losses in stride with laughter.
4. Refuse to grieve over what cannot be changed.
5. Realize the power of a loving God who generously provides the grace to negotiate the way through the curves and challenges.

6. Cultivate an attitude of excitement and childlike expectation over what's in store.
7. Determine to keep it simple.
8. Seek to discover God's best.

As we develop these attitudes, instead of fizzling out, we'll be able to keep the fire.

REFLECTIONS

1. What kind of senior adults were Simeon and Anna?

2. Take a personal inventory of the seven parts of your life which won't stop till you do. What is the condition of your marriage? Spiritual growth? Intellectual development? Physical health? Service? Desire for new experiences? Goal-setting?

3. Set at least one goal for the golden years.

CHAPTER 2

RETIREMENT: THE THREE P'S

PRECONCEPTIONS,

PLANNING,

POTENTIAL

Business Expert:
How many people do you have approaching retirement?

Personnel Director:
Well, we haven't got anybody going the other way.

JAMES BOSTIC

Fred: "Now that I'm retired, I don't do nothing. And I don't start that till noon."

Frank: "Bet you go home early, too."

Fred: "Yep. And a lot of times I find myself going to bed with it only half done. Biggest problem is, I never know when I'm caught up."

These two sedentary seniors typify the fun, fizzle, and flop fraternity. For them retirement can fast become a glass of iced tea, an easy chair, and their favorite soap operas. If they don't watch out, they're gone—literally—in eighteen months.

Then there's the social, sport, and safari set: free folks on a mission. An average day involves rising at the crack of dawn and polishing the clubs for a 7:30 A.M. tee time. Later they'll drop a few bucks for lunch with their golfing buddies. A trip to town or fishing will last till sundown. Dinner, Scrabble, and discussion of travel plans provide a grand finish to a bang-up day.

Theirs is an all-out recreational charge to the finish line. They don't retire, they *retire*. Like high-bred steeds just let out of the barn, they want the exhilaration of running the pasture awhile longer. They yearn to grab the good life. Organized to the max, this breed travel-trailers the U.S.A. and tours Europe. Exotic isles of paradise? Sure! Golf in Hawaii, photo safaris in Africa, snorkeling in the Caymans, fishing in New Zealand—you name it, they're up for it. Go, go, go. Consistently you hear them say with pride, "I'm further behind now than I was when I was working."

Go, go, get 'em, get 'em, or kick back and relax. For many people, getting on in years means adopting one of these mind-sets. Sixty-five equals retirement equals, above all, leisure. The last fifth of life is reduced to a recreational interlude before the sweet by and by.

PRECONCEPTIONS

Retirement, the major response to aging in our society, means different things to different folks. The picture of retirement as a time of maximum leisure and minimal commitment is simply one of many preconceptions people have.

Retirement: What's it to you? For some people, retirement is no more than a fantasy. Financial limitations make the idea of stopping work inconceivable. What else is there to do each day?

Young parents struggling to make ends meet often fall into this camp. They cannot imagine life without struggle and responsibility. "I Owe! I Owe! It's Off to Work I Go!" describes life in the child-rearing lane. These sentiments also sum up the lack of financial security many senior adults experience in our over-mortgaged, credit-dependent society. There seems no end to life, labor, or bills.

Thoughts of death cause some people to view retirement with fear. It is a harbinger of death, the last mile of track before the train stops for good.

For others the idea of retirement brings frustration. All their goals haven't been accomplished. They've never made CEO. They've never spent enough time with their kids. They're not going to write the great American novel, isolate a cure for cancer, get a hole in one (or even make par or break 100). Lost chances, missed opportunities—retirement ignites regret.

For still others, retirement spells fatigue. It promises to be the soft feather bed at the end of a hard day's life. "These are my tired holes," said my retired buddy Ned, an ace golfer, after uncharacteristically triple bogeying a sixteenth hole. For many, that's all retirement is. The tired holes. It's a time for rest, characterized by minimal effort, infrequent exertion, and diminishing ability. Little of significance can or will ever be produced by seniors with this attitude. Their "let up and lay up" mentality says the best years have already been.

Finally, many people anticipate retirement with fascination. They are intrigued by the possibilities that this stage of life, potentially consisting of a considerable number of years, may bring. They're curious. They're searching. They're challenged. With 1980 statistics showing that one may expect to spend some fourteen years—20 percent or one fifth—of one's life in retirement, maintaining such a positive outlook has got to be the best way to go.[1]

Retirement: What It Is and When It Is. You remember the question. You've heard it a million times, a zillion. "Are we there yet?" Our five kids were famous for demanding progress reports from Pearl and me at twenty-minute intervals on vacations. Between potty breaks, of course. And this was supposed to be fun?

"Are we there yet?" is a question about retirement which, in our culture, can be easily answered. Actor Charlton Heston, serving as commercial spokesman for a health corporation, puts it this way, "Retirement—a state of time, not a state of mind!"

While aging may be partly a state of mind, retirement is almost certainly a state of time. Currently the average retirement age in America is sixty-two.[2] Each year, thousands of people reach that age and opt to call it quits, even though they receive reduced monthly Social Security payments. Social scientists predict that the retirement age will be raised to seventy over the next several decades to accommodate the massive baby boom generation. According to A. Haeworth Robertson, former chief actuary for the Social Security administration, baby boomers will on average retire in their early seventies, not their early sixties.[3]

Despite its popularity, it may surprise you to know that the whole phenomenon of retirement is a relatively recent one. People were never expected to retire as we do today. In fact, the designers of Social Security set the national retirement age at sixty-five in an era when life expectancy at birth was only sixty-three![4]

Psychologists B. F. Skinner and M. E. Vaughan write: "Retirement is a modern idea. Until recently, as people grew older, they simply did less and less of what they had always done, or turned to work that was easier." According to Skinner and Vaughan, in 1870 only one-fourth of men in America over sixty-five were not working. By 1970, this number had ballooned to three-fourths! Parents are also "retiring" from their responsibilities sooner than they used to. Years ago when families were larger, parents were often in their sixties before the last child left home. Now when the empty nest is faced, Mom and Dad may be middle-aged, as young as forty-five! "When old age starts that soon," conclude the psychologists, "it lasts a long time."[5]

Retirement: Is It Easy? "We're spending our kids' inheritance!" shouted the bumper sticker on the back of a shiny new motor home. "Take a look at Grandma and Grandpa's new playpen," said Henry, a gleam in his eye, showing his grandchildren the new RV. For Henry and Jane, like so many others, retirement was going to be fun: They'd go north in the summer, see the leaves in the Northeast during the fall, head to Florida for the winter. They couldn't wait!

Despite the eagerness with which retirement is anticipated, it can be tough, especially at first. We spend forty-odd years striving to make it there, only to find the change from job to retirement isn't all it was cracked up to be. Paul Fremont Brown likens his own transition into retirement to "giving birth to a litter of hippos."[6]

We go from enjoying a free weekend away, a free night out, two free weeks, to coping with a free life. The vacation becomes permanent. A life pattern of enjoying times of rest as restorative periods is abruptly altered. Often, as Skinner and Vaughan put it, "those who retire in order to rest soon find themselves anxious to get back to work—and out of a job!"[7]

Is retirement easy? No way! Retirement will be a challenge to most people.

The complexity of retirement lies in the fact that it is both an end and a beginning. It marks the end of years of dedication to a job and the beginning of new opportunities. The search is on to fill our once highly structured and scheduled time.

Retirement is also complex because it affects both individual and family. When Dad retires, Mom's life is dramatically altered, whether or not she also quits work.

Additionally, many of the trials of life, such as serious illnesses and the deaths of spouses and friends, occur more frequently during retirement. True, medical advances are enabling us to generally lead longer, healthier lives. But medicine is also extending life faster than it is slowing the development of such chronic debilitating conditions as arthritis, stroke, Alzheimer's, and related neurological diseases. People are living longer in the nineties but often neither better nor more independently than prior generations.[8]

Not only is retirement demanding because of the adjustments at home and from the job, but it is also destined to become increasingly difficult because of the burgeoning number of retirees in our society. I mentioned in the last chapter that the baby boomers—the generation which once refused to trust anyone over thirty—will come of retirement age over the next two decades. Whoa! That is a whopping half the adults in the United States today! In 1940 the ratio of workers to people eligible for Social Security benefits was 45 to 1. Today it is 3 to 1![9]

Add to this the fact that baby boomers are generally opting for smaller families than their parents. Many boomer marriages consist of double income partners with no children (Code name: DINKs—double income, no kids; or the newest subspecies: DINKWADs—double income, no kids, with a dog). This means fewer and fewer children will grow up to form the work force of the early twenty-first century.

This population shift translates into a smaller labor force supporting a huge contingent of retirees. The Census Bureau reports that by 2005 there will be 114 people over sixty-five for every 100 middle-aged men and women. The Social Security system, assuming it does not go bankrupt, will require massive taxation to service the demands of thousands of aged baby boomers.[10] The quality of life many seniors face in the decades to come will decline from what it is today, even for the most affluent. Future generations of retirees will work longer, have less, and live less independently than their predecessors.

Is retirement easy? No. And it's only going to get rockier.

Retirement: Is It Biblical? Okay, so retirement isn't a piece of cake. But is it biblical? What does Scripture say on the subject?

First, let's consider retirement as the total cessation of labor, a period of several years toward the end of life when the primary focus is on personal leisure and fulfillment. Is that kind of a retirement biblical? You might be surprised at the answer.

In a recent *Time* magazine article, evangelist Billy Graham is quoted as saying, "The New Testament says nothing of Apostles who retired and took it easy."[11]

It is interesting that when King Solomon ran through a litany of human experiences in Ecclesiastes 3, he didn't mention retirement. "There is a time for everything, and a season for every activity under heaven: a time to be born and a time to die, a time to plant and a time to uproot" (verses 1-2 NIV). Nowhere does Solomon mention a time to retire or to permanently cease work.

Retirement is mentioned in only one passage of Scripture, Numbers 8:23-26:

> The Lord said to Moses, "This applies to the Levites: Men twenty-five years old or more shall come to take part in the work at the Tent of Meeting, but at the age of fifty, they must retire from their regular service and work no longer. They may assist their brothers in performing their duties at the Tent of Meeting, but they themselves must not do the work. This, then is how you are to assign the responsibilities of the Levites" (NIV).

Even in this instance the Levites were only instructed to give up certain types of work at age fifty. They could still instruct and assist the younger men.

Many Bible passages extol the value of hard work and perseverance. Again, from the writings of Solomon:

> That every man may eat and drink, and find satisfaction in all his toil—this is the gift of God (Ecclesiastes 3:13 NIV).

> So I saw that there is nothing better for a man than to enjoy his work, because that is his lot. For who can bring him to see what will happen after him? (Ecclesiastes 3:22 NIV). She watches over the affairs of her household and does not eat the bread of idleness (Proverbs 31:27 NIV).

Go to the ant, you sluggard; consider its ways and be
wise! It has no commander, no overseer or ruler, yet it stores
its provisions in summer and gathers its food at harvest.
How long will you lie there, you sluggard? When will
you get up from your sleep? A little sleep, a little slumber,
a little folding of the hands to rest—and poverty will
come on you like a bandit and scarcity like an armed man
(Proverbs 6:6-11 NIV).

All hard work brings a profit, but mere talk leads only to
poverty. The wealth of the wise is their crown, but the
folly of fools yields folly (Proverbs 14:23-24 NIV).

Not only is hard work commended in Scripture, but idleness or laziness, including the lack of a vocation, is spoken of
with disapproval. Some of the early Christians at Thessalonica
evidently felt Jesus' return was imminent and that this gave
them an excuse for a wholesale work stoppage to await Him.
The apostle Paul responded to the issue with these words:

Make it your ambition to lead a quiet life and attend to
your own business and work with your hands, just as we
commanded you (1 Thessalonians 4:11).

For even when we were with you, we used to give you
this order: If anyone will not work, neither let him eat.
For we hear that some among you are leading an undisci-
plined life, doing no work at all, but acting like busybod-
ies. Now such persons we command and exhort in the
Lord Jesus to work in quiet fashion and eat their own

bread. But as for you, brethren, do not grow weary of doing good (2 Thessalonians 3:10-13).

Don't forget that the apostle Paul held down two jobs: tent-making and preaching.

In the Old Testament, a tragic episode from the life of King David illustrates the dangers of too much leisure time. First Samuel 11 contains the account of a fateful spring when kings led their troops to battle. David, middle-aged and too valuable to be risked on the battlefield, sends General Joab to command the troops while he remains behind in Jerusalem.

Unoccupied, bored, David is relaxing out on the roof one night when a beautiful body bathing next door blows him away. Making contact with Bathsheba is easy for a man in his position. Dinner on the roof under the stars with wine and roses sets the stage for seduction. The rest is history—an unwanted pregnancy, an arranged murder, a national tragedy, and the utter devastation of a political family.

Satan loves sitting targets. When we are pursuing life with purpose, he has a harder time distracting us. In Scripture, lifestyles of idleness are never praised. Too much time on our hands spells trouble. Work is both good and necessary.

Does this mean leisure is wrong? Don't even think it! It's okay to take time to play. It's good to rest and relax. The Lord set the example Himself by taking a day off after creating the earth and its inhabitants (Genesis 2:1-3). Relaxation refuels us to keep fighting the good fight.

So what about retirement? It is not wrong, either. Yet I'd have to argue that leaving a job to pursue a life filled only or chiefly with recreation and lacking purpose and direction is biblically and morally wrong! Society may demand we exit the work force at sixty-five or seventy. We may not be able to perform the job we held for forty-plus years. Retirement from an occupation is often a necessary part of life. But it's what we retire to that counts with the Lord!

God has assignments for believers of every age. The job of the Christian life never stops. Retirement from a profession only means more time for a new career: serving Christ. This job puts us on call twenty-four hours a day, seven days a week, for the duration. The pay may not be great, but the benefits are eternal! It's a second chance to answer the call of God in our lives.

PLANNING

Perhaps part of the problem in coping with retirement is that we see it all wrong. We consider retirement a goal, in and of itself. We pour ourselves into life, thinking that a few final years of total freedom will be the well-deserved reward for our efforts. We cheerfully anticipate the opportunity to think chiefly of ourselves at the end.

We should be thinking of retirement not as a goal, but as a phase! It is a developmental stage like childhood, adolescence, young adulthood, mid-life. It's not something to shoot for, but a time of life to be lived to the fullest. It comes with its own rules and lessons. Like every phase, it is to be both enjoyed and endured. It can be an exciting time to do for others what you always wanted to do.

And, if you're smart, retirement is to be planned.

Something of significance rarely just happens. We live with it before we experience it. So it is with retirement. We must plan before we get there.

Daniel J. Levinson envisions each stage of life as a time in which "a man must make certain key choices, form a structure around them, and pursue his goals and values within this structure."[12] You will be making choices as you approach retirement. Even refusing to make a choice is really choosing!

Foolishness is knowing what is coming yet not preparing for it. If we party on a rooftop waiting for the hurricane to blow in, we get what we deserve when the winds and waves crash over us. Failure to prepare is preparation for failure. If we simply wait for old age to bowl us over with its difficulties, it will. The time to start preparing for a fabulous finish is now, no matter how old you are.

Correct attitudes in retirement are cultivated long before retirement. Unhappy people are those who let things happen to themselves rather than make things happen for themselves. They are reactive rather than proactive. The key is setting goals.

Auren Uris suggests that if one is unprepared for retirement, it may be that he or she often has been unable to face up to the facts of life. Afraid of the uncertainties of the future, resistant to the idea of advance planning, such folks arrive at the day of retirement in disbelief that it is really happening to them.[13]

Don't be one of them.

Be prepared to plan, even if you're already there. To paraphrase a hokey saying, this is the first day of the rest of your retirement! Don't let up. Live it up! And set goals in the following areas if you haven't already done so. Your last shot is the best shot you have left.

Vocations and Avocations. Auren Uris calls retirement the "ultimate promotion."[14] So it is. Psychologists advise us not to look at retirement as a "yearned-for rest" or "escape from hard labor," but to choose a career which will allow our involvement to taper off. Often vocational choices do not permit such flexibility, but certainly the avocations we choose can be selected with the idea of retirement in mind.[15] By mid-life, if not before, we should be engaged in meaningful pastimes, learning experiences, volunteerism, and Christian service which will continue after we retire.

Finances and Health Care. According to the American Association of Retired Persons: "Studies show that those who enjoy their retirement most fully have laid careful plans, well in advance, regarding not only finances but also how they will maintain their health in retirement, how they will use their time, and where they will live."[16] The AARP hits on most major areas of retirement that necessitate preplanning: time involvement, finances, health care, housing. Chapter twelve of this book deals exclusively with the financial considerations of retirement. In considering our finances, however, we must not forget that God will provide and is ultimately in control. He will supply what we need. He expects us to be good stewards of that which He gives us, so wise planning is certainly within His will.

Preplanning finances also means being prepared to deal with the issue of health care in retirement. Later chapters discuss this topic more fully, but let me just say that my own parents wished they had done more of this. Mom and Dad moved into a Mennonite retirement home just months before my father, who had battled ill health for many years, died. It took some last-minute financial adjustments on the kids' parts to accomplish this move, but it was comforting to know our eighty-year-old mother was cared for and surrounded by friends when Dad was gone. Some substantive preplanning for finances and health care would have made the transition far less bumpy.

Housing and Time Involvement. Where you will live is an issue that should be settled well before you retire. Tom and Olive chose Austin, Texas, as their retirement site long before it was time to retire. They purchased a home, meticulously wrapped up their affairs, and planned exactly what they would do with their time. It's safe to say they are busier than ever. Both in their seventies, they recently described how many of their friends were compiling family albums of photographs and memorabilia for their children. Joked Tom and Olive, "We're saving that for the nursing home when all we can do is paste pictures!"

For Christians, the vistas of involvement during retirement are limitless, and meaningful involvement is essential. According to J. Campbell White:

> Most men are not satisfied with the permanent output of their lives. Nothing can wholly satisfy the life of Christ within his followers except the adoption of Christ's purpose toward the world he came to redeem. Fame, pleasure and riches are but husks and ashes in contrast with the boundless and abiding joy of working with God for the fulfillment of his eternal plans. The men who are putting everything into Christ's undertaking are getting out of life its sweetest and most priceless rewards.[17]

For each Christian, the question, "How does God fit into my retirement plans?" is vital. Better, let's make it, "How do I fit into God's plans?"

THE POTENTIAL

It is critical to remember that God has a plan and purpose for our final years, as He does for every other stage of life. Just as in our earlier years we grappled to discover the Lord's will for our lives so that we could be in the place of maximum fulfillment, effectiveness, security, and fruitfulness, so now we must consider what He wants for the last half.

Whatever your age, don't buy into the lie that your useful years are behind you. Leaving the work force does not hail the end of significant productivity in your life.

I recently counseled a friend whose life is coming unraveled. I gave him an assignment I hoped would help. He promised to set at least one goal in each of five crucial areas of his life for the next year. These goals are to be realistic and manageable and ones he will be committed to. We are not talking about resolutions. Those can be broken in a minute. We are talking goals.

Would you consider taking the same challenge? Right now, write out one goal in each of the following areas of your life:

1. Spiritual
2. Physical
3. Family
4. Marriage (if applicable)
5. Money
6. Vocational and/or avocational

Keep reading to discover some unique goals God has for the rest of your life as revealed in the ultimate strategy manual: the New Testament book of Philippians.

REFLECTIONS

1. Set the goals asked for at the close of the chapter. Discuss them with your mate, a friend, or a family member.

2. Look again at your six (or five) goals. Which is the most important to you, and why?

3. Look once more at your list of goals. Which one are you going to start working on first? Why?

CHAPTER 3

WHEN IN DOUBT, READ THE DIRECTIONS

*So if you're a Levite priest, according to God's Word
your retirement decisions have been made.
If you're not, read on.*

LARRY BURKETT

Sam recently stepped aside from a powerful position as CEO of an oil company. He was used to issuing orders and having his subordinates kowtow to his wishes. Getting to the top of the corporate ladder hadn't been easy. He'd fought and scrapped his way there. He was a hard worker, no doubt. But it was talent, brains, guts, and drive which elevated him to the upper echelons of his company. His competitive spirit, intense personality, and burning passion for power fueled his achievements.

On the first of January last year, all that dramatically changed. Sam stepped down as chief executive officer. As so often happens when the top guy retires, he took a seat on the board of directors and retained significant shares of stock in the company. But Sam was no longer at the helm, and semiannual board meetings left him with a lot of time on his hands. He relished the opportunity to travel with his wife, Betty, and to really get to know his grandkids (he'd never had time to do enough with his own children). The perks of his retirement package were nice.

Still, things were so different.

At parties, Sam now found himself introduced as the *former* president of X-Oil. He occasionally paid a visit to his old office. The staff made him feel welcome, as did the young bucks now in key positions. Frank, his successor, was always warm and genial. But on each visit there were a few new faces, some changes in the layout. Minor things, really, but pretty soon Sam felt like an old patch on a new pair of jeans.

The other day, Sam's sons converged at the family compound. They asked about his financial arrangements. What plans had he and their mother made in case one of them should suffer a long illness and require extended nursing care? "Mom, Dad, now is the time to talk of these things—while you're healthy!" explained the oldest boy, Pete.

Sam really got upset. He had just gone through all that with his father's cancer and they were still facing it with Betty's parents. He knew he was next in line, but hold on! Not so quick!

Kids. His were good ones—successful, with families of their own. They weren't out of line. They were concerned. But how strange that they should feel they had to check up on things. Almost like they didn't trust their old man.

Sam found something else unsettling. Life had begun to take on a dreary sameness. Mondays used to signal the beginning of a week of challenges. Corporate fires to be put out. Meetings. Friday was wind-down day, if a crisis didn't intervene.

Saturdays were for R & R. Golf, maybe dinner with friends, possibly a reception or party. Now every day seemed like Saturday. No structure. No commitments. No appointments. No schedule. It was as if the teams had chosen up sides and Sam was in the bleachers, watching.

At least Sam didn't have financial concerns. His investments and company benefits would see Betty and him through nicely.

All in all, it seemed to Sam that retirement wasn't what he thought it would be. There was a gnawing sensation in his gut that if this was all there was, the pie wasn't big enough.

CHANGES

Sam's predicament is a common one. Jerry Stubblefield, in *A Church Ministering to Adults,* describes the relationship between retirees and their former careers: "The meaning of retirement cannot be properly assessed apart from the significance of work in the lives of most adults. A person's work has a great deal to do with self-esteem, role in society, economic status, and the whole personal identity. The abrupt termination of work can call for major adjustments in a person's life-style, everyday routines, social contacts, and family relations."[1]

Stubblefield suggests four major problems which confront the suddenly unemployed senior adult. One involves the loss of job-defined roles. Sam, once a corporate heavyweight, is now a former CEO. Others become ex-coaches, professors emeritus, former principals. All the titles mean the same thing: Life doesn't need you anymore. Men and women may find it tough to operate outside the job structure which supported their authority. Redefining relationships is seldom easy.

Typically, Stubblefield observes, a change in professional status also affects home life. When Dad's position as income earner changes, his perception of himself may also change. He may wonder if he will still be respected now that he is unproductive. His wife and kids may be concerned about how he will fit into the domestic scheme of things. Witness the behavior of Sam and Betty's sons. The next generation may feel duty-bound to assure themselves that the folks are acting responsibly and are taken care of.

Third, retired adults face the loss of their job-defined life structure. Life's rhythm of five- to six-day workweeks and short weekend respites is broken for good.

Fourth, Americans generally don't derive self-respect from leisure, so many question what they have done in quitting.[2] Sitting around on one's duff gets old fast.

There are vast changes in attitudes and opportunities retired men and women experience. These can be unnerving at best, and seniors like Sam often have problems adjusting. The difficulties may linger, causing depression and making retirement seem more a life sentence in a self-made prison than a reward. But is this true of everyone?

SURVEYING THE FIELD

Retirement literature is packed with analysis of the problems of senior adulthood. It carefully outlines difficulties with poor self-images, family tensions, social adjustments, physical problems, unmet emotional needs, and strained relationships. These issues must not be minimized. Certainly Sam faced most of them.

Yet as I read about the heavy adjustments seniors must make in retirement, a nagging thought kept coming to mind.

For the past fifteen years I had preached in two retirement community churches. I hadn't usually noticed self-concept problems among the senior adults in the congregations. Even those who had very little in a material sense didn't seem anxious about finances. Marriages seemed to have become stronger with retirement. Relationships with children and grandchildren had, with notable exceptions, improved. There was some loneliness, but not much more than experienced by younger members of the congregations. Worries about mortality and disease were not excessive.

Nearly every time a retirement problem was discussed in a book or article, I found myself thinking, "I don't see too much of this in the churches." Was I ignorant? Mistaken? Insensitive? I wanted to develop more objective data about whether Christian retirees were truly more content than their worldly contemporaries.

We created a survey to be given to retired members of four churches in and around a midsized Texas city. The 111 participants were selected at random from two evangelical churches located in recreational communities largely populated by retirees, and from two "city" churches—one affiliated with a major denomination and the other non-denominational. While the survey was limited in size and scope, its results should be of value to all of us who are preparing for our senior years or working with this age group.

At first I thought the senior adults in the retirement communities would prove to be better adjusted than the urban seniors because they had probably planned more extensively for their later years than their urban counterparts. "Not!" as my grandkids would say. There was no appreciable difference in the survey responses. Scratch one theory!

THE FINDINGS

Considering the volume of books detailing the agonies of quitting the work force, problems of self-image and self-worth associated with retirement seemed insignificant among the men and women I surveyed. Sixty-seven percent said they never worried about no longer being employed. Only 11 percent said they often worried that they no longer contributed meaningfully to society. The vast majority had no such concern.

Five percent of those surveyed often worried about adjusting to a lower standard of living, the same percentage that regularly contemplated returning to work. Over half had no concerns at all about changes in their living standards.

Togetherness seemed to be the rule for the married participants. Ninety-five percent spent significant daily time with their spouses, and 84 percent expressed affection to their wives or husbands every day. Relationships with children and grandchildren also seemed strong.

Socially, the seniors surveyed seemed well adjusted and content. Loneliness was never a problem for over 70 percent. Only 5 percent often felt socially left out. Most saw retirement as a blessing in which additional time allowed for such choices as travel, associating with relatives and friends, recreation, and hobbies. Over 90 percent found the time "to do as I please" to be a major blessing of retirement.

What were the concerns of our seniors? Over half worried at least some of the time about declining health and debilitating and catastrophic illnesses. Twenty percent worried often about finances related to health care; 45 percent found this a sporadic concern. Very few worried about death, and most of the apprehension centered around the fear of dying after a long illness. Eleven percent felt anxiety about the possibilities of dying and leaving their spouse or children with debts.

Spiritual matters seemed of paramount importance to the group. Nearly all said they prayed daily, attended church services regularly, and frequently contributed to the church. Seventy-three percent indicated they read the Bible daily, and nearly that many said they often volunteered for church activities (meaning they attended fellowship functions as well as accepted positions of service).

How did these seniors say they chiefly made use of their time after retiring?

Activity	Percent replying
Recreation/hobbies	86
Watching TV	85
Reading books	73
Volunteer work	50
Visiting sick and shut-ins	39

Over 85 percent of those surveyed often spent time recreationally or watching television! Half did volunteer work often. Just over 33 percent regularly visited the sick and shut-ins, but in a separate section of the questionnaire, 44 percent indicated they were often concerned about changing society and the world.

QUESTIONS

The final page of the survey contained two questions which I hoped would provide additional insights. The first was, "What has been your biggest adjustment [to retirement]?"

Many of the concerns discussed by authors of retirement literature were mentioned. Initially there were problems with changing roles, self-image, and relationships with family and friends. Typical responses included these:

> I found I wasn't able to do as much as I used to.
> I had trouble adjusting to less income.
> Not having a rigid work schedule was tough.
> Too much togetherness was difficult at first!
> I had trouble deciding how to spend the extra time and set priorities.

According to the survey results, such concerns were short-lived.

The second question was, "What losses do you feel the most?" Typical responses included:

> I miss seeing my friends.
> The loss of my parents was hard.
> I miss the business relationships.
> My relatives are all dying.
> I miss being able to work as hard as before.

The losses of family members and friends are inevitable passages of life and not necessarily linked to retirement. Missing work and work relationships, on the other hand, is a direct result of exiting the work force.

WHAT DOES IT MEAN?

What can be made of all of this? When all the surveys were tabulated and the work had been done, I realized I was having a refreshing experience. These people, for the most part, were happily adjusted to their new way of life. They had made the transition from work to retirement quite effectively.

Some of the retirees even offered solid, upbeat advice concerning how to make this transition. One section of the survey encouraged participants to write down questions they wished had been asked, complete with their own answers. A few of these bear reprinting:

Question: What is your overall opinion of sixty-five and up?
Answer: It is the greatest and God is so good.

Question: Is your life richer now and more fulfilling?
Answer: Yes.

Question: Do you have a positive attitude toward retirement?
Answer: Yes, a positive attitude toward retirement is
        important. It should be regarded as a new field of
        endeavor, a new challenge to pursue and to enjoy. My
        philosophy is that if you enjoy what you are doing, it's
        not work, and I've never worked a day in my life.

What terrific attitudes to beat retirement blues!

CONCLUSIONS AND CHALLENGES

"I've always had the best of life," wrote a survey participant. "I do hope all the positive answers haven't messed up your research!" She should be assured, they haven't.

To the contrary, the results were an inspiration to me in many ways. They were also a source of challenge.

Remember, the surveys indicated that the vast majority of these seniors were vitally interested in spiritual matters. Most were active churchgoers who prayed and contributed to their churches regularly. Nearly half (44 percent) expressed frustration at not being able to change society and the world. Clearly, our retirees were interested in God and in doing something for society. Yet how were they spending their vast amounts of free time? In evangelizing? In teaching God's Word? In studying Scripture?

Perhaps our retirees were engaged in these pursuits, but over 80 percent listed recreation, hobbies, and watching television as their frequent pastimes. Only half reported that they often did volunteer work.

The deep spiritual interest expressed by most of the seniors cannot be ignored. Neither can the desire of so many to significantly impact society.

For the Christian retiree, there is great potential to do much more than simply engage in leisure activities. Most of those surveyed are building family relationships. Most are engaged in spiritual activities. But the untapped potential in those areas is still amazing. There is, as in all of life, room for so much more! Stubblefield observes: "Retired men and women can bring a rare combination of gifts to the mission and ministry of the church. They have wisdom hammered out on the anvil of experience, technical knowledge and skills derived from a variety of occupations and large measures of discretionary time. They represent an enormous pool of human potential, waiting to be utilized in the service of God."[3]

A successful transition to retirement signals that we are ready for so much more. Life goals do not end at sixty-five. We need them at all stages of life. Goals for godly living. Goals for serving God. And in the case of senior adults, goals to finish well. God has a lot for us to do: Things that are spiritual, things that will impact the world, and things for eternity. Who says it better than the apostle Paul? "Run in such a way that you may win" (1 Corinthians 9:24). "I have fought the good fight, I have finished the course, I have kept the faith" (2 Timothy 4:7). Not a bad eulogy for any of us.

Psychologist Paul Tournier asks, "How can a person who has completed his working life and who has arrived at the time of retirement, renew himself for the third age of life?"[4] The call is for us to become more concerned with *production* than *reduction* in senior adulthood. No matter how old we are, as Tennyson would put it, "Death closes all; but something ere the end, / Some work of noble note, may yet be done.... 'Tis not too late to seek a newer world."[5]

People who aim at nothing generally hit it, and retirement is no exception. God has a better idea. The psalmist wrote: "The length of our days is seventy years—or eighty, if we have the strength; yet their span is but trouble and sorrow, for they quickly pass, and we fly away.... Teach us to number our days aright, that we may gain a heart of wisdom" (Psalm 90:10,12 NIV).

What counts at retirement is how we make use of it. How do we determine our priorities? The older we get, the greater should be our concern that we are in vital pursuit of what is important to our heavenly Father. Relatively little has been written about retirement as it relates to God's plan for this period of our lives. Questions like these must be answered: What is the Lord doing in my life? What are His objectives for me? What is my job description now? How should I look, act, and be?

The apostle Paul answered these questions and others in his letter to the church at Philippi.

A LOOK AT PHILIPPIANS

The book of Acts tells us how Paul, on his second missionary journey, ran out of real estate when he arrived in Troas with Silas, Timothy, and Luke. They tried to go in several directions, but the Holy Spirit restrained them. While at Troas, Paul had a vision of a man from Macedonia appealing for help.

The next morning, Paul and his traveling companions booked passage on a boat north to Neapolis. When they landed, they set out on a short hike to Philippi, where a businesswoman named Lydia became a follower of Christ.

But there were problems. Midnight found Paul and Silas beaten, bruised, and battered in a Philippian prison. They prayed and sang songs of praise to God. A heavenly rumble was heard. The earth shook, the prisoners' chains were loosed, and one scared jail guard assumed the worst. He knew his prisoners must have escaped, so he drew his sword to kill himself. There was no room for errors or acts of God in his job description.

But no. Paul, Silas, and the others had not flown the coop. The Philippian jailer couldn't believe it. He and his entire family came to faith in the Lord Jesus Christ as a result, and the church was started in Philippi (Acts 16:14-40).

Paul came to love the Christians at Philippi. They were his baby church. Bosom buddies. Close friends. Years later when he wrote the thank-you note and love letter we call the book of Philippians, he was in dire straits himself, in prison once more. Paul's letter is intimate, personal, straight from the heart. It deals with controversial issues, but it is also full of friendship, gratitude, conviction, character, and compassion.

Most authorities believe Paul wrote Philippians when he was confined in Rome, probably under house arrest.[6] From Philippians 1:20-26 it is clear that the apostle felt his future was uncertain. He didn't know if he would live or die.

As it is with senior adults, it was apparently late in the race of life for Paul as he wrote. Everything was up for grabs. He wasn't exactly a senior citizen, but he knew the palpable reality of looking death squarely in the eye. Rome's mad emperor Nero was not known for his charity work or awareness and sensitivity training. Paul's life in prison in Rome hung literally in the balance, dependent upon the whims of a ruler who had not hesitated to have his own mother executed. Not a nice guy, Nero.

While the traditional view holds that the apostle would be released from his Roman imprisonment for a short period of time, he didn't know this when he wrote to the Philippians. The letter, to best of his knowledge at the time, was likely to be his last. We know Paul's thoughts were on the finish of life because he wrote of being poured out like a drink offering. He said that to depart and be with Christ was appealing but that he was determined to stay on for the sake of the churches. He wrote of finishing the course, keeping the faith, receiving the crown.

What is your "prison," as you approach senior adulthood? What limitations are you facing? Depression? Physical infirmity? Emotional upheaval? Financial anxieties? Fear? Uncertainty? Does your life seem to be on production hold, slipping toward the finish with little promise of fulfillment? Are you searching for significance? The apostle Paul could relate to that. As he wrote Philippians, Paul wanted to be able to hit the reverse button and relive some of the good times or fast forward and go home to be with the Lord. But it seemed as if God had hit the pause button. Paul was experiencing many of the negatives of the golden years: isolation, financial stress, limited social involvement, health problems.

Because Paul was confronting the finish of life, he could write with conviction about what really matters. The important. The essential. The end of the line was just ahead. His days were precious.

In his letter, we find instructions to see us to the end. We probably won't be imprisoned, awaiting possible execution, but we will likely face our sixties, seventies, and eighties with the growing recognition that life on earth has its restraints and is flying by quicker than we can stand. Paul told his readers, and by application us, how to go out in a blaze of glory. There was no "quit" in him, as a South Texas rancher might say. Wouldn't you rather finish well than fizzle out? Paul gives us the guidebook.

THE GOAL OF CHRISTLIKENESS

It is the Father's purpose, when we come to know Jesus Christ as Savior, to begin a work in our lives using every means possible to make us more like His Son (2 Corinthians 3:18, 1 John 3:2). The believer's ultimate goal? Simple: to cooperate with the Father's purpose of making us more like His Son. Cooperation with the Father is a lifelong process that does not end with retirement. Our pursuit of the spiritual disciplines should never stop.

Think about it. As we near the finish line, we have the opportunity to cooperate even more fully with God than earlier in our lives when other demands weighed heavily upon us.

We've got the time! Yesterday's priorities no longer distract us. Earning a living no longer consumes us. Retirement can be a marvelous occasion for God to put the finishing touches on our lives so that the world will see Christ in us.

In his intimate letter to the Philippians, Paul outlined ten goals for godly living to help us demonstrate authentic Christlikeness. They are worthy goals for Christians at all stages of life. We'll consider them in roughly the same order they are presented by Paul in Scripture:

1. Loving with the love of Jesus
2. Living for the glory of God
3. Confronting life one day at a time
4. Remaining stable in the storm of suffering
5. Being a servant
6. Knowing Christ intimately
7. Keeping the joy
8. Maintaining an effective prayer life
9. Planning financially for a Christlike finish
10. Depending upon the adequacy of Christ all the way home

It is my hope that applying to retirement God's purposes for life outlined by Paul in Philippians will correct our orientation and help us not to focus on personal comfort and selfish pursuits during the precious final years. Instead I hope to challenge each of us to honestly ask ourselves these questions: What does the Father want of me? How can I cooperate with His goal of making me more like Jesus?

You are somewhere in the process of becoming like Christ if you are a child of God. God's own Spirit is exposing you to a curriculum designed to produce Christlikeness in you. Your choice is to bend and blend in with God's plan or to buck and blow it. So often in twentieth century America we have gone far afield of the goal of Christlikeness. Even in the church, we have become consumed with the creature rather than the Creator. God never promised to make us healthy and wealthy, but He does promise to give us wisdom if we ask for it (James 1:5). The ultimate manifestation of this wisdom is to become more like the Son: "Therefore, since we have so great a cloud of witnesses surrounding us, let us also lay aside every encumbrance, and the sin which so easily entangles us, and let us run with endurance the race that is set before us, fixing our eyes on Jesus the author and perfecter of faith, who for the joy set before Him endured the cross, despising the shame, and has sat down at the right hand of the throne of God" (Hebrews 12:1-2).

THE BEST IS YET TO BE

Gail MacDonald dedicates her book *A Step Farther and Higher* to her husband, Gordon, with these words:

> To Gordon,
> my climbing partner
> of twenty-eight years:
> Together we have
> loved the peaks;
> Together we have lived
> through the valley.
> Together we will see
> The best is yet to be.[7]

The best is yet to be for senior adults, too. Spike White, founder of Kamp Kanakkuk in Missouri, says he outlived all his canoe partners and took up kayaking at age seventy-two. Now he has run the Colorado River through the Grand Canyon and conquered America's ten best rivers for the sport.[8] On her ninety-third birthday, Miss Lucy Webb of our Hide-A-Way Lake congregation made a list of ninety-three things for which she was thankful and presented it to her Bible study teacher. The list ran the gamut from "Jesus" to "heaven, poems, washing machines, and beauty operators." My wife, Pearl, told her, "Miss Lucy, I want to be just like you."

Friends, to paraphrase Yogi Berra, it ain't over till it's over. No matter how old we are, we've got a lot of life left and God has big plans for us.

REFLECTIONS

1. What is your overall opinion of life at sixty-five and up? Discuss your answer with someone. If you are married, be sure to do so with your spouse.

2. Think a moment of one thing God may desire for you to do during your retirement. What impact, if any, will this activity have on your life? On the lives of others?

3. Is there some way you are feeling the limitations of senior adulthood?

CHAPTER 4

THE FRIENDS AND FAMILY NETWORK

LOVING WITH THE LOVE OF JESUS

"I'd die for you, my love."

"O Harold. You're always saying that, but you never do it."

CHARLOTTE, TO SCHILLER

In *The Late Show,* her treatise on growing older, *Cosmopolitan* magazine editor Helen Gurley Brown quotes the advice of psychiatrists Mildred Newman and Bernard Berkowitz: "In marriage, or in any partnership (1) Don't expect to be sane all the time. (2) Don't expect your partner to be sane all the time. (3) But only one of you can be crazy at a time!"[1]

In retirement, both you and your spouse might feel just a little kooky. Suddenly there's an immense amount of time to spend together. Many retired spouses clutch at their marriage, the single area of life they still think they can control.

As one church member put it, retirement may just be "half as much money, twice as much husband, and three times the grief."

THE HEART OF THE MATTER

Relational shifts occur in the healthiest of marriages, families, and friendships as we mature. The upheaval is more pronounced when the person retiring hasn't maintained solid connections with spouse, children, extended family, friends, and God. Such a person's life may be shortened. Statistics indicate that divorced people have a significantly higher death rate than their married counterparts.[2] The same seems to be true for lonely, relationship-barren folks.

By contrast, people who reached their late eighties and early nineties in the retirement communities where we ministered nearly always had a strong network of family and friends.

At the heart of it all is love. The kind of love that stays put in the storm of demands placed upon it. Living out such love is the first goal that will help us run the last laps of life well.

As we show our love in our relationship to God, He produces in us the love capable of standing the test of time with our spouse. Then love is extended to our family, friends, church, and the rest of the world. Therein lies the rub, for love *among seniors* and extended to others *by seniors* is sometimes missing.

We do too little loving. Of our wives. Our husbands. Our children and grandchildren. Our relatives. Our brothers and sisters in Christ. Our friends, neighbors, and the unsaved world. We do not love long enough, strong enough, or without strings.

Yet believers are commanded to love throughout Scripture: "And walk in love, just as Christ also loved you, and gave Himself up for us, an offering and a sacrifice to God as a fragrant aroma" (Ephesians 5:2). "Beloved, let us love one another, for love is from God; and every one who loves is born of God and knows God. The one who does not love does not know God, for God is love" (1 John 4:7-8).

Real love—God-honoring, gut-wrenching, self-sacrificing love—is the hallmark of the committed Christian life. It is a product of the Spirit of God, who indwells every believer.

The apostle Paul talks a lot about love. It is one of the first subjects in his letter to the Philippians, and its theme permeates the entire epistle. When he wrote to the Philippians, Paul's situation wasn't too different from that of a modern retired adult. Reduced income, restricted physical choices, the possibility of death—Paul experienced all the negatives of the "golden" years while imprisoned.

He took his lumps and losses, but he never stopped loving. We can learn a thing or two from him.

FOR THE LOVE OF JESUS

Paul starts his letter with love, reminding the Philippians of his great affection for them. He continually thanks God each time he remembers them (1:3). He prays for them with joy (1:4). He is confident that the Lord will keep on working in their lives to make them more like Jesus. "Being confident of this, that he who began a good work in you will carry it on to completion until the day of Christ Jesus" (1:6 NIV).

The Greek word translated "carry it on to completion" conveys the idea of *fully* finishing. *Finis.* The end. When we enter God's great workshop, we find nothing bears the marks of haste or incompleteness. God is more interested in working *in* us than *for* us, and He finishes what He starts. You never hear Him saying to a believer, "I'm outta here."

Physical age is no sure indicator of spiritual maturity. Nor does it matter how much time has passed since conversion. Just because we are getting up there in years doesn't mean we have grown up to be like Jesus. Becoming more like Jesus means learning to love without conditions and to give freely of ourselves.

Daily we have the opportunity of allowing the love of Christ to flow through us. It should excite those of us who are approaching our sixties, seventies, eighties, or beyond, to realize that although we are playing in the fourth quarter, there is still time to grab the ball and make a positive contribution for the Lord. Games are often won or lost after the two-minute warning. There may not be *as much* time, but there is always *enough* time, for God's purposes to be accomplished through us.

FROM THE LOVE OF JESUS

While Paul prays for his Philippian friends, he longs for them "with the affection of Christ Jesus" (1:8).

The affection of Christ. This is love in its purest form. The Greek word used by Paul for "affection" is *splanchnon* (splak-non). The Authorized King James Version translates the word "bowels." It refers to a feeling from the viscera, the gut (where the Greeks believed emotions originated). *Splanchnon* is the love which ignites compassion and moves one to action and involvement in the plight of another. It is the love which spurs the Samaritan to aid the bloodied traveler and prompts the father to embrace the prodigal son. In creation's consummate object lesson, *splanchnon* moves the God of the universe to step into human history by sending His only Son to live and to die.

For love's sake, Jesus stretches open His arms and allows Roman nails to split flesh and tendon. His body shudders in agony as the cross is lifted rudely and jolted into place. Flesh rips as His raw back scrapes against the rough-hewn beams. And there He hangs from morning on. Muscles tearing, joints separating, organs swelling, blood pooling in His extremities, His strength is spent staving off suffocation. Sweat and blood mix to matte His hair and beard. Pain written in the pallor of His face, His head hangs bowed as He readies to depart His broken body.

From noon to three o'clock, the Father snuffs out the lights of heaven. The scene is too private, too personal. Blackness shrouds the cosmos while the Son of Man loves us enough to undergo the supreme deprivation of all: separation from God the Father to be made sin for us. For love, Jesus dies for us.

And why wouldn't He? For love, He had already lived for us, surrendering the splendors of heaven to be reviled and rejected by a ruined creation. And love, God's unfathomable love for us, would raise Him again, stamping an eternal seal of approval on the sacrifice of the Son.

It is for love. All for love.

KNOWING IT

Paul, despite his limitations, longs to convey the authentic love of Christ to his friends in Philippi. The apostle looks outside himself and beyond his circumstances to reach out in compassion to touch others. It is only a letter, but what a letter! Full of encouragement, empty of self-pity…it is the love of Jesus in action.

How can we show Jesus' love, too?

Let me state what may be obvious. Before you show it, you gotta know it. You cannot demonstrate the love of Jesus in your life if you do not know Him personally. Jesus' sacrifice on the cross is a hollow act for you if you do not believe that His death took the punishment which you, as a sinner, deserve. "For the wages of sin is death, but the free gift of God is eternal life in Christ Jesus our Lord" (Romans 6:23). Jesus experienced isolation from the Father—spiritual death—so that we would not have to.

Although we don't have to experience spiritual death, tragically, millions do. Among the hardest things for seniors to accept is that salvation is a gift by grace (God's unmerited favor) through faith, and not based upon human performance (Ephesians 2:8-9). We are used to doing things on our own. We admire fierce independence. We like to think we can achieve anything, even heaven. As one senior replied when I asked about eternity, "If I don't get in heaven, it's not fair because I've done pretty good." But Scripture says our goodness is nothing more than a pile of smelly sweat socks, rotten cotton, in God's eyes (Isaiah 64:6). He accepts us dressed in His righteousness alone (Romans 3:23, 5:8).

The reality that even decades of leading a relatively good life do not qualify you for heaven must be digested if you ever hope to demonstrate the love of Christ. If you are not absolutely sure you are a Christian, please read chapter nine of this book carefully. It is late in the game, and your destiny hangs upon your response to Christ. If you are confident of your salvation, the rest of this chapter is for you.

Showing It

We know Christ's love motivated His death for us. What else does Christ's love look like? Try this: "Love is patient, love is kind, and is not jealous; love does not brag and is not arrogant, does not act unbecomingly; it does not seek its own, is not provoked, does not take into account a wrong suffered, does not rejoice in unrighteousness, but rejoices with the truth; bears all things, believes all things, hopes all things, endures all things" (1 Corinthians 13:4-7).

This is the kind of love which the Spirit of God can produce in believers' lives. This is the kind of love that makes all who know us glad they do. It is the love which shatters senior stereotypes and makes for model marriages, firm families, and unbreakable friendships in the retirement years. When authentically displayed before a watching world, it is the love that convinces all of the truth of the good news of Jesus Christ.

In the life of a Christian, Christ's love is the love that meets the needs of others without regard to self:

It is the love that puts a friend's needs first.

It is the love that makes an old man tenderly care for the Alzheimer's-stricken wife who no longer knows his name.

It is the love that prompts an elderly woman to stand by her man while he is walking through the valley of the shadow of death, knowing full well there is a fork in the road and their ways will part, never again to intersect this side of glory.

It is the love which reaches out to embrace a young couple who've relocated far from home.

It is the love which gives generously, selflessly, anonymously.

It is the love which never tires of teaching or serving.

It is the love which unclutters schedules, shifts priorities,
    consumes time, focuses energies.
It is the love which plans for the future, even as the Lord
    has gone ahead to prepare a place for us in eternity.
It is the love which changes lives.

Dr. Ralph Sockman, well-known Methodist minister and author, says, "Love is a force from within seeking expression and not a vacuum waiting to be filled."[3] Why not make it a goal of your senior years to be a vessel filled with Christ's love? You can allow the Lord to transform you into a channel expressing His affection. It's too easy as we get older to become selfish and demanding, to let our needs take priority over the needs around us. The call of Christ is to keep picking up the bucket and towel, washing feet, serving, loving. That's what He was doing, only hours before the cross. Love never quits. It sacrifices and serves till life stops.

HOW? RIGHT ATTITUDES AND REFIRED LOVE

At retirement, most people have the time and opportunity to love more tangibly, more frequently, more effectively than in their professional days. Retirement creates opportunities to refire passion, devotion, and concern in your marriage and other relationships. In Philippians, Paul provides a living object lesson in powerful living and loving through the strength of God's Spirit. What did he do? Three things: He prayed for people (1:4). He saw them as precious (1:8). He encouraged them to be pure (1:10).

Prayer is indispensable in the Christian life. When offered on behalf of others, it is a display of Jesus' love. Paul deals with prayer later in his letter (4:6-7), and to do it justice, we will, too. Let me just say for now that I know of few more effective ways to demonstrate Christ's love than to pray with and for others. Meanwhile, let's look more closely at the two other ways of loving mentioned by Paul.

1. Seeing People as Precious. Scripture says Paul loved his Philippian friends and prayed for them because he considered them precious (1:4,8). The feelings were mutual, as an accurate rendering of Philippians 1:7 reveals: "Even as it is right for me to be feeling this way about all of you, because you are holding me in your heart" (author's translation). Notice, the Philippians held Paul in their hearts even as he cared for them. What did they do? They shared in his work. They stuck by him despite the stigma of arrest. They supported his ministry with their money. They stayed true to what he had taught them.

How do you hold people in your heart? You esteem them. You believe they are significant. You support them. You consider their needs before your own. You show how much you appreciate them. You consider them precious.

This verse taught George and Gladys a lesson. When George came in for counseling, it was obvious his marriage to Gladys desperately needed repair. Neither partner still truly valued the other. Their problem wasn't a lack of self-esteem; it was too little other-esteem. I prescribed some defibrillation to get love pumping again.

"How long has it been since you told Gladys you loved her?" I asked George.

"I dunno."

I urged him to do so and also encouraged cards, candy, flowers, communication, and prayer. The glow on his face the next time I saw him signaled that the old things still work, even after forty years. George badly needed to demonstrate to Gladys that she was precious to him. Today they are as happy as two pigs in the sunshine. Grateful to God and grateful for each other.

No matter your age, look around at your marriage. Husband, how long has it been since you told your wife you loved her? When was the last time you took her to dinner? When did you last sacrifice some of your time, personal preferences, individual desires to serve her? Is she precious to you?

And, wife, what about your husband? Does his presence irritate you? Is he always underfoot? What are you doing to understand and ease the tremendous transition he is making from the work force? When did you last tell him you were proud of him or otherwise encourage or affirm him? Have you reminded him lately of all he has done to make life so wonderful now?

If you are not yet retired, what are you doing, in love, to prepare for this most challenging time of life? What is your game plan? You can win in life when facing a lopsided score, but you must have a strategy.

Look around at your relationships with your children. Do they know how much you care? Are you showing them how to age gracefully? What about your grandkids? What can you be doing to positively impact their lives? How can you let them know they are significant to you?

What about your friendships? Are you being a friend instead of just having friends?

At your church, are you letting the younger ones do all the work, teach all the Sunday school classes, handle all the youth activities? You can show Christ's love by contributing in many areas and demonstrating to others in your church family that they are significant!

How about the other people you know? Whom can you tell about Jesus? Whom can you assist in some way? Open your eyes to the possibilities! Better yet, turn your eyes upon Jesus and then, after looking at Him for a while, focus on those around you through His eyes. You'll see ways to love that may not have occurred to you before.

Don't fall victim to the stale litany of excuses: "I've done my time. I did all that when my kids were small. I'm tired." If my seventyish buddy Tom Paulk can run in a three-legged race with a bunch of Sunday school kids, you can surely give an hour each week to teach memory verses or Bible stories. You can hold a suffering friend's hand or read Scripture to a bedridden neighbor. You can ask a newcomer to lunch.

If your church has all the helpers it needs (and I've never yet run across one that does), most parachurch organizations are crying for volunteers. You can be constructively involved in the lives of others and find fresh meaning for your own, even while you demonstrate the love of Jesus.

At the core of every act of unselfish service is love. Christlike love manifests itself in actions that meet needs. It lets people know how important they are to us. It reminds them of their significance to Him. Look to Jesus, then look for opportunities! See people as precious.

2. Pursuing and Encouraging Purity. No one really remembers when it started—who slighted whom. Maybe it began with that row over the hymnals. Or did they first argue about flowers in the sanctuary? Or did one hear something the other supposedly said about her? Soon they only communicated through mutual friends.

Whatever its origin, the conflict between the two women was a slowly oozing blister on the church body, a relentless irritant to the spiritual health of the entire congregation. They were both highly visible leaders—one the president of the women's organization; the other, the lead soprano in the choir. Separately, they were delightful ladies who could charm the socks off you. Together...well, let's just say their claws emerged. If they became hysterical and historical at the same time, watch out!

Do you know them? Not likely, but you probably know a few like them. Every church I've run across has at least a couple (it always takes two). The one at Philippi was no exception. There, bound up in the struggle for their own rights, were Euodia and Syntyche. Paul mentions them by name in Philippians 4, where he urges others in the church to help the pair resolve their conflict.

Earlier, perhaps with the turmoil of these two women in mind, Paul had made a plea for purity: "And this is my prayer: that your love may abound more and more in knowledge and depth of insight, so that you may be able to discern what is best and may be pure and blameless until the day of Christ" (1:9-10 NIV)

It was a call for sincerity and innocence. A call to surrender of self for others. A call to love.

I don't know why Euodia and Syntyche had trouble getting along. I can only guess that one offended the other somehow. Minor resentments festered. Lines were drawn, sides set. When two are locked in a struggle for personal pride, a match can go fifteen rounds. Folks get beaten up and bruised. Nobody wins. The results? Strife. Competition. Defensiveness. Division. Slicing fellow saints stifles the Spirit's work.

In my years of pastoring, I have often observed gross instability in relationships among seniors. Little things tragically demolish friendships. Minor rifts become major chasms. Friends of thirty-odd years refuse to speak to each other because of disagreements over the way the church should be run, what the pastor should do, how the sanctuary should look.

At one church, half a congregation might have made a mass exodus if we hadn't been careful about doing away with a fireplace during an expansion program! No kidding! Choices about color schemes, art work, literature, pledge cards—you name it, we survived the controversy and kept growing. But there were plenty of power struggles and battered feelings along the way.

How easy it is to squander vast emotional energy on relatively insignificant issues. Too many seniors must bear responsibility for the strewn wreckage of fragmented relationships they really didn't care about maintaining.

Younger Christians are not immune to conflict. But more often, in my experience, it has been the older ones who succumb to the temptation of demanding things go their way. Resistant to change, some view anything new as liberal, suspicious, or from the devil. As one senior put it while discussing suggestions for the church music program, "We've always done it this way and God told me He would like us to keep doing it this way!"

Why is it often so hard to encourage and pursue purity in relationships as we grow older? Perhaps freed of the demands of child care and career, many seniors simply have too much time on their hands. Change may well be tougher for retirees to handle, too. They are less geographically mobile than younger members of congregations, more used to the way things have always been, more threatened by adjustments in routine.

Then again, senior selfishness is often the natural outcome of a life that has been spent selfishly. Retirement only magnifies selfish behavior which has always been there.

The primal allure of power cannot be minimized, either. At any age, the temptation to grasp power instead of giving love can be nearly irresistible. Henri Nouwen suggests that this may be because power is an easy substitute for "the hard task of love." It becomes easier to "be God than to love God, easier to control people than to love people, easier to own life than to love life." Historically in the church, we are more concerned with sitting at the Lord's right hand than with loving him.[4]

No matter what the reasons, the bottom line is this: What kind of love are we displaying if we discard friendships and marriages callously and conveniently, like so many used-up Kleenex?

In nearly every situation I have encountered, when horizontal love is shallow and fleeting, it is because there is a problem with vertical love. When two people have a problem with each other, usually at least one of them has a problem with God. So often we see this in senior Christians who have given up on spiritual growth. When men and women throw it in spiritually as well as vocationally, difficulties spring up like weeds in an untended lawn. When we stop seeing to our own spiritual development, we use the time to tend to others. We search for crab grass in the garden of a brother and miss the stinkweed in our own.

Paul wanted none of this! He wanted the Philippians' love to overflow. Think of a bucket standing underneath a gentle waterfall. Liquid fills the pail and spills over the rim. This ought to be a picture of our Christian love for one another, especially as we age.

Asa and Billie know it. They live it. As they've grown older, the economy has damaged the family business they started. No matter. They keep on loving. Both are dealing with physical infirmities but continue thinking of others. The first person I recognized after my hip replacement surgery was Billie standing by to be sure I was okay. Asa? He keeps hanging in there, sharing hugs, words of encouragement, big smiles no matter what. They are real lovers. Ask anyone who knows them.

FALLING MORE DEEPLY IN LOVE WITH THE SAVIOR

Paul wanted the Philippians to "discern what is best" so they would be "pure and blameless" before Christ (1:10 NIV). He knew that if their love was right for Jesus Christ, they would know how to act. They would know what offends Christ and what doesn't.

As we fall more deeply in love with the Savior, we detect behavior in ourselves which is not Christlike. Because of this love, we correct our behavior. We change. We grow. We learn to do the right thing at the right time in the right way, and in so doing, we become more like Jesus Christ.

This is what Paul longed for Euodia, Syntyche, and all the rest. He hoped they would test their conduct against God's example and standards. The word translated "pure" in Philippians 1:10 suggests being sun-tested. In Paul's day, during the manufacture of porcelain, pieces often cracked. These defects were revealed as the craftsman held up the pottery to the sunlight. He would then fill in the cracks with wax. In a similar way, God holds his children up to the light. He looks for the "cracks" in our lives and hearts. He searches for cracks in our commitment, motivations, love. "For the eyes of the Lord range throughout the earth to strengthen those whose hearts are fully committed to him" (2 Chronicles 16:9 NIV).

Paul yearned for his friends to withstand the sunlight test! He longed for them to be open and honest before others and God. He wanted them to get a queasy feeling in the gut when something was wrong. He wanted them to respond in love to what God taught them. He wanted them to love God more deeply than any habit, practice, or preference. He wanted change to issue not from their own efforts, but from a deepening love relationship with the Father. He desired that they be fully prepared for the coming day of Christ.

This day of Christ is an occasion when we who know Jesus will stand before Him. At this event, also called the judgment seat or *bema*, we who sowed bountifully, lived unselfishly, and loved sacrificially will enjoy a time of joy and reward. Believers who did not will want to shrink away in shame, watching everything they have done go up in smoke, though they themselves escape the flames (1 Corinthians 3:12-15, 1 John 2:28).

Our lives must be pointed toward that culmination, the day of Christ, rather than settling for a phony climax at retirement.

A SPECIAL WORD FOR MARRIED SENIORS

It's true. I married over my head. People always like me better after they meet my wife. If she sees something in me, there must be something to see. We are each other's biggest fans, and we've been together a long, long time.

There is an extraordinary potential beauty and unity in mature wedded love. Comedian Bill Cosby says a man and wife aging together are "breaking down in tandem."[5] Who better remembers what you used to be than your spouse? If you've been married twenty, thirty, forty, fifty years, you share a common history of joys, sorrows, struggles, and successes. You've reared your children and maybe even been blessed with a few grandchildren and great-grandchildren. You've seen it and done it and lived through it all. There's no reason why your final years together can't be your best yet. Psychologist Paul Tournier calls mature love a "prefiguration of heaven" because it is less tumultuous than youthful love, less directed toward selfish pleasure-seeking, more inclined to result in clear understanding and communication.[6]

Poised at sixty-five, you're about to pass "Go" and collect the bonanza of a busy, bountiful, passionate old age with the one you love.

That is, if your marriage survives your retirement.

Many don't, even though as Helen Gurley Brown puts it, "Extricating yourself from marriage is about as comfortable as getting yourself removed from a tub of wet cement…and a lot more expensive."[7]

One old buck was said to have filed for divorce at age ninety-six. When asked why it took him so long, he explained, "We wanted to wait till all the kids had died."

There's a ring of truth to that. Countless couples aren't committed to each other for the long haul. Many stumble near the end and lose the reward that could have been theirs.

Sometimes retirement proves to be the final straw breaking a marriage's back. Two couples I attempted to counsel divorced shortly into retirement. Their cases were strikingly similar. When it came time for the husbands to retire, four marriage-busters rose from the past to kill the present, destroying both relationships:

1. Separateness. Work and child-rearing had never been joint efforts, but sources of conflict and division. There was seldom a sense in either marriage of "We're in this together" or "No matter what happens, I'll be here!"

2. Unfaithfulness. By one or both partners, infidelity in earlier years set the stage for bitter, explosive retirements. In one case, the indiscretion occurred after retirement. The widow across the lane needed and appreciated her neighbor's help, and before either knew it, they were in each other's arms.

3. No common interests. Neither couple spent significant pre-retirement time developing mutual likes. Pearl and I have a list long enough to last into eternity of things we want to do before we are done. Our interests are so diverse that it has taken no small effort to arrive at this common ground.

4. Lack of spiritual unity. No matter how trite it may sound, when you pray together, you stay together. Common commitment to Christ, worship, and prayer is glue that makes a couple stick. I'll always remember praying side by side with Pearl in our dating days. After the "Amen," I kissed her for the first time. Wow! Call the preacher! Set the date!

A year later we were married and there have been forty anniversaries since. We've been blessed with a quiver full of five kids and are going on seven grandchildren. We have traveled a rocky road at times, but our marriage has grown because of a four-lettered word: not *love*, but *work* in the marathon of love. This means hammering out compromises, choosing alternatives, setting aside preferences—all with the purpose of glorifying God.

Five years ago Pearl and I sat down nose-to-nose for forty hours to honestly evaluate our relationship. We wished we'd done it years earlier! I learned that I eat too fast and drive too fast, and that I am a real jerk. (Not Pearl's choice of words—she was kind.) The experience was eye-opening, ego-busting, and worth every minute.

Unfortunately, Richard Steele's caustic assessment of marriage as "the compleatest image of heaven and hell we are capable of receiving in this life"[8] frequently becomes all too real at retirement. One survey showed over half of the wives of retired men (and two-thirds of the wives of early retirees) actually regretted their husbands' retirements.[9]

What a contrast this trend is to Solomon's advice on marriage in Ecclesiastes: "Enjoy life with your wife, whom you love" (9:9 NIV). Too often, as the country song goes, "It's too hot to fish. It's too hot to play golf. And it's too cold at home!"

Retirement is no time to walk out on a marriage. In thirty-five years of ministerial counseling I have never run across an entirely hopeless situation. Many come close. But, with God involved, nothing is so tough that it cannot be worked out if the parties are willing.

BUSTED OR BROKEN?

As soon as Frank came to the little church, he was a force to be reckoned with. Within a week everyone knew that he had served on elder boards at other, *big* churches and that he had spearheaded fund-raising for major building projects. Frank had once directed internal affairs for a large conglomerate. It became obvious that retirement had left him a frustrated executive who dearly missed running the show.

Before long, Frank campaigned for a seat on the town council and won. He also became the self-appointed bishop of the little church. Demanding, critical, perfectionistic, convinced of his own correctness, he didn't make things easy for anyone. Following one of Frank's tirades, a weary friend asked him, "Are you planning to go to heaven?"

"Yes!" Frank replied.

"Don't bother. You won't like it."

To folks like Frank, retirement is a bust. It isn't so great for those surrounding them, either.

But with people like Robert, it's another story. His life was the story of sacrificial giving and unselfish loving. A diagnosis of advanced cancer meant Robert wouldn't be with us long. I started spending an hour or two with him weekly to help him prepare for the end. His wife, Marjorie, sat in on one session and said, "Thank God we don't have to make up for lost time in our marriage, because we have loved each other deeply all our lives and we have demonstrated it freely."

This priceless couple's retirement was hardly a bust. They allowed themselves to be God's vessels, pliable in His hands, broken if necessary. They were always ready to love and were greatly loved in return. Robert died recently, but Marjorie keeps on going, despite her enormous loss.

May we all be sacrificial lovers just like them.

May we, like a vial of precious fragrance at the feet of a King, be willing to be broken and spilled out so that we might love just a little as Christ loves.

REFLECTIONS

1. Learn the ways God has uniquely gifted you. Make your relationship with Him top priority.

2. If you are in midlife, check your marriage. Beware the jolts and creeping separateness which derail relationships. If your eulogy were written today, would it say what you want it to say about you as a husband or wife?

3. Consider your other relationships. How would you be remembered if you were gone tomorrow?

4. Think about your spouse, a neighbor, or friend. What are three tangible ways you can demonstrate to this person that he or she is precious to you?

5. Consider the people you know in your church. Are there any Euodias or Syntyches in the bunch? Can you be a peacemaker in that situation? Will you pray for the problems and the people?

6. Honestly, how are your relationships with others in your church or neighborhood? Are there some bridges which need to be rebuilt? Some fences to mend? Some areas in which you are determined to have your own way, no matter what? Are you willing to flex, to yield your prerogatives for the sake of the relationships?

CHAPTER 5

WHOSE LIFE IS IT ANYWAY?

LIVING FOR THE GLORY OF GOD

𝓇

*The man who lives by himself and for himself is liable
to be corrupted by the company he keeps.*

DON HEROLD

One Easter Sunday, Luella watched her beloved husband, Woody, confess his faith in Christ. It was among her happiest moments. Not that marriage to Woody had been bad. Rarely had I seen two people so obviously in love. A geologist, gourmet cook, and irrepressible humorist, Woody added spice, love, and a good deal of fun to every life he touched, mine included. Retirement was a joyous adventure for both of them...until tragedy struck.

Shortly after trusting Christ, Woody was diagnosed with terminal cancer. His death after a long, painful struggle with the disease devastated Luella. Her life seemed robbed of meaning. Luella refused to give up, instead looking to God for strength to keep up the business of living.

Woody had been Luella's gift, her joy, her lover, her friend, but the Lord Jesus was and is her life. Today Luella is as warm and vibrant as ever. An international traveler, serious

Bible student, infectious laugher, committed hugger, dedicated pray-er—Luella enriches the lives of all she knows.

Ruth was just the opposite. As we walked down the hospital corridor far enough from her husband's room so that we might talk openly, Ruth's bitterness and fear exploded in words of despair. Like Woody, Mark also was dying of cancer. From the depths of her grief, Ruth cried, "He is my life! If Mark dies, I will have nothing to live for!" Within six months of Mark's passing I preached at a second funeral, Ruth's. It was a double tragedy. Ruth had nobody and nothing left to live for.

Luella understood, but Ruth never learned, this secret to a fulfilling life: Live for someone or something greater than yourself. Woody was vitally important to Luella. No one could have loved a man more. But he was not her entire reason for being. For Ruth, life was Mark. She was ill prepared to cope with his loss. Unable to function without him, she gave up. Soon she too was gone.

WHAT MOTIVATES ME?

As you approach senior adulthood, ask yourself, for whom and what am I living? Is it a marriage, a job, a house, a dream? Children or grandchildren? Leisure, recreation, sport? Television, church, music, food? Whatever you live for, will it last?

Sid lived for his job. His life was consumed with the goings and comings of the office. When he retired, Sid missed the work environment so much that he sank into a deep depression which only was alleviated when he found part-time employment. He was overqualified for the new job, but he was working!

For Betty, life is her house. She sees it as an extension of her person. Colonial decor and antiques grace every room.

Marge lives for tennis. Really. She plays every day, often twice a day. She takes lessons and attends clinics, referees and plays in tournaments. She is the secretary of her seniors league and the hospitality chairperson at the club. Her friends are, of course, tennis players.

For R.J., life is golf. Clubs, clothes, carts, and scorecards consume him. Spare moments find him in lessons, on putting greens, at driving ranges. His VCR hums at night with videos of the golfing greats. His two goals in life are to make a hole in one and to shoot his age for eighteen holes.

Actually there were many in our retirement congregations of whom this was true. I always joked that I preached to kick-offs and tee times! Woe was me when my sermon ran over and the Dallas Cowboys kicked off at noon!

Living for a pursuit, a career, an avocation, even a church are simply ways of living for ourselves. There is nothing wrong with recreation, relaxation, and rest. There is nothing wrong with devoting ourselves to a hobby, sport, or other avocation. But there is a problem when these activities become the sum total of our existence, our reason for being! Then life lacks deeper meaning and purpose. What really counts is missing.

Living for ourselves ultimately yields bitter fruit! We require a higher calling.

C. T. Studd, a missionary to Africa who gave up fortune and family to spend himself for God, said, "If Christ be God and died for me, there is nothing too great that I can do for him."

As Christians we must ask ourselves, "For whom or what am I living?" The utter abandonment of ourselves to Jesus

Christ is a vital step toward Christian maturity. It is never too late to begin living for the glory of God, no matter what.

The apostle Paul knew what it was to live a life sold out to Jesus Christ. He knew what it meant to stay flexible so that the Father might function through him. He knew what it was to long for the peace of death and heaven but to choose the struggle of earth and life as long as it pleased God to keep him here. Motivated by the love of Christ, Paul knew what it was to live for the glory of Christ! And living for God's glory is goal number two for running the last laps of life well.

SEEING OBSTACLES AS OPPORTUNITIES

George and Mary Jane have few of the world's goods, but you'd never know it. A postman's pension doesn't leave much room for extras. Expensive dinners out, theater tickets, and hefty green fees are occasional treats for the couple. Vacations abroad, exclusive clubs, and costly jewelry are beyond their reach. Some of their peers wonder if doing without ever gets to them. But it would never occur to the teenagers in the Sunday school class George and Mary Jane teach that this couple lacks anything. It doesn't occur to George or Mary Jane, either.

George and Mary Jane live life with a larger goal in view. They dance to a different beat. The path they have chosen is that of the Savior. They know that to really live you've got to give. They live for the glory of Christ.

A fixed income is but one of the limitations George and Mary Jane have experienced in retirement. Most senior adults confront limitations of some sort as their years increase. We must adjust to the loss of power, prestige, and control that comes from exiting the work force. The older we get, the more debilitating disease is likely to strike us, our parents, our loved ones. The longer we live, the greater our chances of getting sick. People don't die of good health.

Indeed, as Barbara Deane notes, retirement in the 1990s may mean some things that no one tells you about:

> Caring for aging parents
> Helping out adult children
> Coping with your children's divorce and remarriage
> Having to raise your grandchildren
> Facing widowhood and remarriage[1]

Like senior adults, the apostle Paul faced limitations as he wrote Philippians. Under house arrest, his movements were restricted, contact with co-workers diminished, finances questionable, and future uncertain.

But the apostle wrote that his "circumstances have turned out for the greater progress of the gospel" (1:12). How? Simple. A detachment of the praetorian guard was assigned to Paul. The guard, ten thousand elite troops loyal to the emperor in Rome, was a crack outfit that received double pay and special privileges. Paul found himself with literally a captive audience as the guards were chained to him for six-hour intervals. He must have talked their ears off, telling them about Jesus: "This isn't my first time under arrest you know. Ever hear about what happened when my buddy Silas and I were in jail in Philippi? Little earthquake rumbled. The cell doors popped open. We all could have walked. Easy. But we didn't. We stayed put so the chief jailer could keep his head. You know who made that earthquake? God. The God of the universe who loves you and wants to have a relationship with you. Let me tell you about Him" (see Acts 16:25-31).

For Paul, prison equaled progress! The gospel spread, despite his limitations and scant resources. The gospel spread because of his chains! His pulpit was the prison; his congregation, his captors. Since Paul allowed God to use his confinement, news of Christ spread throughout the praetorian guard (1:13). From there it could easily have been conveyed to highly placed military and government officials. Via transfers and troop movements, the gospel was likely taken by common soldiers to the very ends of the Roman Empire—the far reaches of the known world.

All this occurred because Paul saw not the opposition, but the opportunity. He didn't see chains; he saw chances. He saw advantage in adversity. He made a conscious decision to live for the glory of Christ no matter what.

George and Mary Jane have made a conscious decision to let some of the stumbling blocks of their senior years become stepping stones, too. Finances limit how much traveling they can do, so they use the fact that they are "stuck" at home to minister to others. They never miss a Sunday at church. They visit the teens they teach. They attend the high school football and basketball games and root for their "kids."

George and Mary Jane are the first to be called when someone goes to the hospital because they will be at home and available. They encourage their children and grandchildren to visit for extended periods. They pick up mail and newspapers and water the plants for their traveling friends, never complaining that they are not the ones sending postcards.

They've got too much to do. And an army of teens will rise up in heaven one millennia to praise the impact George and Mary Jane have had on their lives.

LEAVING A LEGACY

Something else happened as the apostle Paul kept talking about Jesus. Other Christians saw Paul's example and were encouraged to follow suit (1:14). News of Jesus spread.

Paul might have been handcuffed, but God cannot be restrained. The slogan of the toughest survivors is often, "I can't do that anymore, but I can still... " We back up, but we don't give up. We let God do through us whatever He wants, however He wants.

When we are around people who have every human reason to throw in the hand and cry "Misdeal!" yet are still playing with enthusiasm, we can't help but be inspired. In my younger days I was ready to quit at the sixteen-mile mark of the Las Vegas marathon. Exhausted, dripping with sweat, dehydrated, I thought I was finished. Along came a seventy-nine-year-old man, jogging in old slippers tied to his feet. He passed me. Needless to say, I completed the race, but not ahead of him. He inspired me to keep running.

Whom might you inspire? What will be your legacy with your kids? Your grandkids? Godly seniors can be tremendous examples to those who follow!

Those of us who have grandchildren know that they are smarter, cuter, more graceful, more athletic, and more insightful than their parents ever were. As Al Onkin put it, "My grandson recites the Gettysburg Address and he's only nine. Lincoln didn't say it until he was fifty."

Barbara Deane observes that grandparents fill important functions in family life. They support their children's transition into parenthood, acting as stabilizing influences. They also moderate conflict and lessen the abrasiveness of family life by giving both generations a "safety valve." They connect the present with the past by communicating family history and traditions to those who follow.[2]

The family framework is falling apart on many fronts, and increasing numbers of grandparents are pressed into a second tour of duty, raising their kids' kids. Prison wasn't a pleasing prospect for Paul, but he saw in it possibilities for the progress of the gospel. If you find yourself in round two of child rearing, accept the challenge as an opportunity given by the Lord to use all the wisdom you acquired in round one.

Pearl's stepmother, Lillie, did this, and made an incredible contribution to the lives of her grandchildren Rhonda and Dower. Both of these precious kids are grown and now have families of their own, but it never would have happened if Lillie hadn't graciously accepted the call and toughed it out daily with joy.

FOR GRANDPARENTS ONLY:
SIMPLE WAYS TO SHARE JESUS

A vital function of Christian grandparents is to impart spiritual truth to their grandchildren. Grandparents have unique opportunities to share Christ and see the gospel spread among those they love most. Here are six ways you can share Jesus in your family:

1. The rules are simple. Life is always more important than lip, walk than work, conduct than creed. Relational evangelism means I love, serve, and stay involved to earn the right to share

my faith. When you have withstood time and tests and have earned their trust, introducing your grandchildren to Jesus may be as easy as picking ripe fruit that practically falls off the tree into your hand.

2. Barbara Deane and others recommend that seniors let their children and grandchildren really know them. Suggestions include letting yourself be interviewed by family members, and making cassette or videotapes of yourself recalling childhood memories, family members, and events. Great idea! My own family is poverty stricken in this area because the day my dad spontaneously reminisced about family history for my youngest daughter, no recorders were rolling. Now Dad is gone and the memories are lost.

When you preserve family history, don't leave out the spiritual dimension. Be sure to include the account of your conversion. How did you come to know Jesus? What has He meant to you over the years? What sort of religious heritage did your family have?

3. Take the grandkids to your church with you occasionally. If they live at a distance, invite them to visit you during summer vacation Bible school. The kids will be kept busy part of each day, making your time together less taxing, and they'll receive eternal benefits from the lessons and activities at church.

4. Invest in a week for your kids, grandkids, and yourself at a Christian family camp. Dottie Austin and Asa and Billie Hollemon have done this over the years with eternal dividends. Nothing is more hilarious than watching and hearing Dottie and her large clan playing Frisbee golf...and little is more moving than seeing several generations of one family celebrate communion together at the close of camp.

If family camp isn't possible, try sending your grandkids to a quality Christian children's camp. Your financial assistance would likely be a great help for parents struggling to pay for braces and mortgages! After a fun-filled week, the children will probably be willing to earn part of the camp tuition themselves the next year. Again, the dividends will be eternal. According to a 1990 survey by Christian Camping International, half a million individuals currently engaged in full-time Christian service made decisions to follow Christ at Christian camps!

5. Build a good library of Christian videos the grandchildren can watch when they come. Send some home with them for further viewing.

6. If your children object to your sharing your faith with their children, back off. You've bumped into green fruit. Keep praying. Your time will come. Trust God and watch Him work.

You probably have plenty of time for these important relationships in your senior years. What you do with it reflects whom you are living for! You can see the progress of the gospel in the glorious years ahead of you, if you want to. In fact, your senior years have the potential to be your most fruitful! "Even when I am old and gray, do not forsake me, O God, till I declare your power to the next generation, your might to all who are to come" (Psalm 71:18 NIV).

STICKS AND STONES

Pearl and I knew we were getting older when our children started to look middle-aged. As Bob Dylan would put it, the times they are a changin' for us all.

Perhaps harder than living with the limitations of maturity is dealing with the attitudes others may adopt toward us.

Suddenly our children, although well-meaning, don't think we can handle things like we used to. They encourage us to sell the house for simpler digs, say a retirement apartment or senior center. They may pressure us to move nearby (which may or may not be a good idea depending upon your relationship). Other times it may seem our kids have forgotten us. As they get busier with their own children and careers and we have more time on our hands, we can easily feel neglected, especially if they forget special occasions.

In planning the future of the organization that coordinates my ministry work, our board members sometimes speak of me as if I had one foot in the grave and the other in ICU. I think my skin is thinning as the years go by, just like my hair. I swear I heard a couple of them arguing at the last meeting about who would get to be my pallbearers. About all that's left is planning the hymns and speakers for the service!

Like many my age, I'm discovering that with maturity comes both constructive and destructive criticism.

Our own parents, if they are still living, may demand increasingly large chunks of our time and patience as they develop special needs. We may experience criticism from other relatives about how we treat them. Our choices may be called to question. One friend is still facing condemnation from siblings about her choice of a nursing home for their dad. A widow I know has not yet overcome the guilt she feels about her husband's death and her choice of physicians.

The division of family property is another matter. Problems multiply as estates are divided. Sisters and brothers may question our motives. Many families split after the parents are gone.

Additionally, a culture which encourages us to devote ourselves to pleasure trivializes us. It minimizes our importance by turning us out to pasture and denying we have anything to offer past sixty-five. Of course there are always those who will seek to exploit our age and fears, too. Investment, insurance, and sales scams often target seniors, who are considered vulnerable.

The apostle Paul understood all this, too. He was criticized, exploited, even back-stabbed. He wrote that some people, hearing of his imprisonment, preached Christ out of "envy and strife," and "selfish ambition." Their purpose was to cause Paul "distress" (1:15,17).

Hidden agendas are everywhere, even in the kingdom of God. Critics tried to stop Nehemiah from rebuilding the wall around Jerusalem (6:1-3). The apostle John caught flak from Diotrophes (3 John 9-10).

Alexander the coppersmith stuck it to the apostle Paul (2 Timothy 4:14-15). So, evidently, did some folks in Rome who professed Christ but preached about Him out of jealousy. They must have thought their success bothered the apostle. They wanted to show Paul what they could do without him.

And he didn't even care. Like John the Baptist, Paul was willing to decrease that Jesus might increase (John 3:30). He accepted it all for the glory of Christ: "What then? Only that in every way, whether in pretense or in truth, Christ is proclaimed; and in this I rejoice, yes, and I will rejoice" (Philippians 1:18).

Sticks and stones may break my bones, but words will never hurt me. We all know the children's rhyme isn't true. Words hurt. But Paul didn't let words get to him. He refused to become bitter, angry, frustrated, vengeful. Instead he focused on the results: Christ was preached. He rejoiced.

So can we if we focus on how the gospel of Christ can be spread through what we are enduring and how we are living.

TO GOD BE THE GLORY

Buttressed by the prayers of believers and the strength of God's Spirit, Paul was confident of deliverance (1:19). Regardless of the outcome, the apostle had only one consuming life purpose—to glorify God: "According to my earnest expectation and hope, that I shall not be put to shame in anything, but that with all boldness, Christ shall even now, as always, be exalted in my body, whether by life or by death" (1:20).

What matters? The glory of Christ—that's all. When we have surrendered to His sovereignty, He does with us as He pleases. He lives and works through us. When confronting the limitations and losses of senior life, we too can say, "What does it matter?" if we follow these principles:

1. *See the progress of the gospel taking place through what is happening to us.* Retirees Charlie and Marie know a thing or two about that. A horrific accident on an interstate highway landed them in the hospital. The elderly aunt traveling with them was snatched instantly to heaven. Charlie very nearly died in the emergency room. Marie spent the next several months convalescing. Was it worth it? Oh, yes, because among other miracles, the couple's son came to a saving knowledge of Jesus Christ.

2. *Believe others are affected by our attitude.* A whole church was driven to its knees by Charlie and Marie's trial. The

congregation prayed round the clock for their recovery. Every hospital visitor returned with stories of inspiration about the couple. Folks who had hoped to encourage Charlie and Marie found themselves encouraged by the godly couple's calm acceptance of the situation.

The standing ovation greeting Charlie and Marie on the Sunday they finally returned to church together was more than a welcome home. It was an acknowledgment of all the ways they had blessed the congregation during the ordeal—a collective, "Thanks for the memories."

3. *Have the God-given willingness to turn loose of what needs to be let go.* "God has taught me the meaning of Romans 8:28," said Marie as Charlie hovered between life and death in the emergency room following the wreck. She lived the fact that God was working it all out for good—His ultimate good. Confident of God's goodness, Marie could let go of Charlie.

Living for the glory of God means we surrender our lives to the One who can do it up big and do it up right.

Living for the glory of God means seeing our circumstances as designed by Him for our maximum growth and His ultimate glory. He supplies all the grace we need to go through it.

Living for the glory of God means honestly saying, "Lord, break me! Make me! Fill me! Use me!"

When we are living for God's glory, retirement becomes an opportunity for each of us to catch a fresh view of the goal. We may need to rearrange our priorities, drop unneeded baggage, and increase our intensity for the home stretch.

Are you ready for total involvement in the cause of Christ? Does nothing matter to you except His glory, His honor? Paul was determined his body would be the theater in which Christ's glory would be displayed. Paul S. Rees asked, "What matters? Really nothing, if only the sheer greatness, the unutterable bigness of Jesus Christ, somehow breaks through and becomes luminous in this frail physical frame."[3]

"I said to the LORD, 'You are my Lord; apart from you I have no good thing'" (Psalm 16:2 NIV). Truly, what else matters?

Senator Robert Desmond, commissioned to make a study on the problems of aging, made the following retirement recommendations:

1. Start planning your retirement in your thirties and forties.
2. Don't stop working abruptly; slow down gradually.
3. Make useful activities the core of your retirement plans.
4. Develop an interest outside your business or profession that you can use when you retire.
5. Devote part of your time to civic or charitable service.[4]

To that list we might add, consider asking this question about everything you plan for your future: "How will this bring glory to Jesus Christ?"

Vernon Grounds recounts the story of Thomas Edison losing his great New Jersey laboratories in a raging fire in December 1914. The next morning, walking among the charred remains of the buildings which had housed so many important projects, Edison, sixty-seven, was heard to say, "There is great value in disaster. All our mistakes are burned up. Thank God we can start anew."[5]

For all of us determined to live for the glory of God, senior adulthood may just be the new start we've been seeking.

REFLECTIONS

1. If you are in midlife, make financial decisions now which will keep you free from heavy debt as you enter retirement years.

2. Think about ways your vocational skills, gifts, and abilities could be used for the glory of God.

3. What keeps you from staying focused on Christ? Start lightening the load today.

4. Have you recorded family history and traditions as a legacy for your children and grandchildren?

5. In what ways did God use Paul's confinement to His glory? How might the Lord use the circumstances of your senior adulthood to spread His gospel?

CHAPTER 6

STAYING STABLE IN THE STORM

THE SUFFERING OF CHRIST

𝄢

No pain, no palm; no thorns, no throne;
no gall, no glory; no cross, no crown.

WILLIAM PENN

E rma Bombeck describes her feelings following breast cancer surgery with just two words: "road kill." Her stitches, she writes, resembled a road map of Kansas with only one main highway.[1]

When I saw the staples for the first time following my hip replacement, I was convinced I had my own B & O Railroad. Tracings of the Oregon Trail lined my stomach. A treasure map X marked the spot where the old hip once was. Buried there in its place was a new, shiny hip that would set off any sensitive airport security system.

The nice thing about aging is when you want to lose a little weight, instead of going on a diet you can just check in and give them another part you won't be needing for the rest of the trip. I've definitely reached what they call the metallic age: silver in the hair, gold in the teeth, lead in the britches, stainless steel in the joints. But so far my plate has been relatively empty of the gut-wrenching, heartbreaking suffering of some dear friends...like Pat Guion.

In 1985 Pat's husband, Donnie, a Dallas engineer who had served fifteen years on our ministry's board of directors, underwent a routine physical. The exam revealed a spot on his lung. What? It couldn't be! Donnie had never smoked a day in his life. Within six months he was gone, the victim of virulent cancer. We wept with Pat, her children, and grandchildren. It wasn't supposed to happen this way.

Pat is a survivor. She found healing support in the Lord, her family, friends, and church. Attractive, vibrant, positive, generous, she showed us all how to rebound from a shattering loss. Then she faced a trial all her own.

Few of us noticed that Pat fasted the last day of our ministry's spring 1990 board retreat. Tests the next morning at a large Dallas medical center showed a suspicious mass, and surgery was recommended. Pat insisted the operation be performed the next day. She saw no reason to go home and prolong things. The verdict? Cancer. Within a few brief years of Donnie's death, Pat was stricken.

Surgery, experimental drugs, and chemotherapy have so far proved effective with Pat. Liver scans are encouraging. Still, as with all serious illnesses, the final chapters are yet to be written.

THE SUFFERING QUOTIENT

Suffering is a given. It strikes us all sometime, somehow. It always has. Read these accounts from three New Testament Christians and weep:

Peter: Beloved, do not be surprised at the fiery ordeal among you, which comes upon you for your testing, as though some strange thing were happening to you; but to the degree that you share the sufferings of Christ, keep on rejoicing; so that also at the revelation of His glory, you may rejoice with exultation (1 Peter 4:12-13).

Paul: For I consider that the sufferings of this present time are not worthy to be compared with the glory that is to be revealed to us (Romans 8:18).

James: Consider it all joy, my brethren, when you encounter various trials; knowing that the testing of your faith produces endurance (James 1:2-3).

Christ never promised the Christian life would be a Caribbean cruise to glory on a glassy sea. Physical suffering is more like a rough ride on a fast river. Rocks, rapids, sink holes, trees—the challenges are unending. It is a constant struggle simply to keep your head upright. Just as you hit swift, smooth water, your ears hear the roar of the rapids ahead.

Suffering is no respecter of persons, knows no age limits, acknowledges no boundaries. However, since in senior years we will have lived longer and experienced more, our suffering quotient will probably be higher than in our younger days. A suffering quotient is kind of like a heat index or wind chill factor. Meteorologists use these weather tools to tell us why we feel colder and hotter than temperatures indicate. So it is with suffering. Each difficulty seniors encounter is added to the store of sufferings past. We hurt more than we think we ought to because the cumulative effect of our sufferings is overwhelming. Even a small setback may make us want to crumble.

The kicker is that the setbacks of our senior years aren't usually small at all. This is the time of life when really big health problems clobber us. This is when most people who will be attacked by such diseases get cancer, cardiovascular disease, stroke. Even if certain afflictions like arthritis and Parkinson's disease strike in earlier years, they worsen with age. A retired buddy puts it this way, "When the tires go bald and the mileage gets up there, you can expect some pit stops for maintenance." Our suffering quotient may sail off the charts.

Bad habits of a lifetime frequently catch up with us as we mature. Osteoporosis bends bodies starved for calcium. Smoke-damaged lungs develop emphysema. Overworked hearts give out. Alcohol-abused bodies wear out.

Disabilities may strike with no known cause. My good buddy John Mackinnon was the picture of health. Lean, athletic, a health food enthusiast and avid tennis player, John did it all. He wrote a success story in business and was a beloved teacher of the Word who deeply loved his Lord.

Yet all his healthy living did not protect him from the ravages of ALS, Lou Gehrig's disease. Impossible! Not with everything John had left undone! He was needed badly. He had too much to live for. For a time John's diagnosis was in doubt; a cure seemed possible. Through a miraculous chain of events, comedian and humanitarian Jerry Lewis arranged for him to see the top ALS specialists in the world. But nothing was able to halt the devastation. John died after a lifetime of good health at age fifty-seven.

It was neither expected nor fair.

An old fellow took his radio to the shop and said, "It don't sing no more." That time, physically, is coming for each of us one way or another. The valves start sticking, the pistons start slapping, the hoses break, and before long, we are a steaming mess on the shoulder of life's freeway.

Senior suffering isn't simply physical. That would almost be too easy. We also may experience isolation and transitions within and outside the family. Finances may be an issue. The co-insurance won't pay like it ought to. The pension is inadequate. We may be forced to move and start over again.

Our adult children often face struggles during our senior years. True, they are on their own, but their marital, financial, and child-rearing problems affect us. The older we get, the older our own parents get, too. These years may well be the time they need us most.

We will suffer the loss of friends and family to death and eternity. As a pal grimly joked of his retirement community, "This place is just a holding pen for the funeral home!" With advancing age, wedding and baby showers are few and far between. There comes instead a seemingly endless procession of funerals and memorial services. We ache because of our loss, and sometimes because we are not the one who's gone home.

Whoa. Sounds depressing doesn't it? It needn't be. Remember: Our God reigns! Yet reality should prompt us to throw off what Stephen Sapp calls the "Pollyanna attitude toward aging current in Christian literature—a perspective that fails to seriously recognize the real losses human beings suffer as they grow older."[2]

Life ain't always pretty.
Sometimes the radio don't sing no more.
But always we have choices.

SUFFERING 101

May I suggest something revolutionary? Since suffering is inevitable, why not add it to the goals you have for senior adulthood? The only really grown-up Christians are those who have known the suffering of Christ and who understand that God has a purpose for allowing pain.

Suffering 101 is part and parcel of the divine curriculum for developing Christlikeness. Professor Paul outlines the course in Philippians. We first experience the love of Christ, then we long to live for His glory. Yet we never fully live for the glory of Christ till we are prepared to share in the sufferings of Christ.

We must rethink our ideas about what it means to suffer for Christ. Often in the Christian life we pigeonhole or categorize suffering; there is suffering for Jesus and just plain suffering. Folks who die martyrs' deaths, give up material goods to be missionaries, catch malaria on overseas mercy trips, are persecuted because of the gospel, endure insult because of biblical stances on social issues—these people are suffering for Jesus.

Most of us seldom or never suffer in such ways. But no matter who we are, how we live, or where we live, we will suffer. The challenge is to perceive our everyday trials and tribulations as opportunities to suffer for the Savior.

Stephen Sapp's recommendation is that we take an alternative Christian approach to our expectations of aging, an approach that will "give a central place to the discipleship of the cross, recognizing that the cross Jesus Christ bids his followers to take up includes the ordinary everyday sufferings of human life."[3] This includes age-related difficulties. An honest recognition and acceptance of the losses of aging, Sapp contends, can lead us to accept our "utter dependence upon God, a necessity in the Christian scheme for restoring the relationship with God that has been disordered by human pride."⁴

That means seeing even the garden-variety losses and difficulties of life as sufferings ordered by a loving God to be endured for the sake of Christ and His righteousness. It's *how* and *with whom* we sail through stormy seas that matters, not the size and severity of the waves. In the eye of the storm, we might just look up and see Jesus walking on the water toward us. Or maybe He'll awaken, stand, and shout, "Peace! Be still!" The fact that He is with us means more than anything.

Our daughter Becky would agree with that. Becky is only in her thirties, but has been severely diabetic since age thirteen. She has lived Suffering 101. She wrote these words about a very difficult time in her illness: "I recall when I was on dialysis and my eyesight was getting worse, I expressed my fears of being blind to Ray [her husband], and I'll never forget his words, 'Honey, I know that would be hard on you, but all it would mean to me is that I'd get to walk a little closer to you.' This not only reminds me of God's unconditional love, but it also reminds me of the way suffering lets us 'walk a little closer' to God."

Now a nine-year survivor of a kidney transplant, Becky's health is fragile, her very existence often tentative. I'm her dad and I'm prejudiced, but I can tell you she walks a little closer to God than most of the folks you meet. Suffering has sensitized her to Him and to the hurts and needs of those around her.

Is suffering what we want? No way. Of all choices, it is probably last on the list. We'd much prefer health, material abundance, and the assurance that death will come peacefully in our sleep after we have reached a very advanced, yet mentally alert old age. Even so, suffering can develop Christlike character as nothing else in our lives.

The apostle Paul could tell us a thing or two about suffering. He wrote that during his career as a missionary he was forced to endure imprisonment, severe beatings, shipwrecks, near drownings, stoning, sleeplessness, homelessness, muggings, hunger, criticism, cold. "Apart from such external things, there is the daily pressure upon me of concern for all the churches," he wrote (2 Corinthians 11:28).

The bruised and battered apostle knew what it was to endure wracking loss. Yet he could still write the Colossian Christians, "Now I rejoice in my sufferings for your sake" (Colossians 1:24).

Paul rejoiced that he was able to experience suffering for the cause of Christ and the sake of fellow Christians. If Suffering 101 were an elective course in the Christian life, Paul would have signed up. He would have paid to take it. His sweatshirt would say, "Press Till You Pay! No Pain, No Gain!"

We, too, will have no choice but to suffer somehow as we mature. How we respond to what's ahead will determine whether or not we are suffering for Christ. As a hurting friend commented the other day, "I've learned not to ask, 'Why?' but to ask, 'What is He teaching me?'"

The apostle Paul knew life could be a sloppy stomp through a swamp full of alligators. He gave some keys for sailing above the circumstances—not just surviving—in the final verses of Philippians 1.

REMEMBER WHOSE YOU ARE

The apostle Paul reminded his readers to whom they belonged, urging them to "conduct yourselves in a manner worthy of the gospel of Christ" (1:27). The verse might also be translated, "Live as citizens in a manner worthy of the gospel." The idea is for the Philippians and other Christians to remember whose they are and whom they represent.

When our five kids were teenagers, we'd caution before letting them loose with friends: "Remember, you're an Anderson. Don't forget you represent our family." Usually it worked. (At least we think it did.) Paul gave the Philippians similar instructions: Remember you are Jesus' representative, a citizen of His kingdom. Act like it.

Our friend Pat Guion, who is fighting cancer, lives like a child of the King. She sums up her outlook on life this way: "We have a choice to make each day. Mine is to recognize that this is the day the Lord has made, and I will rejoice in Him." A self-admitted weeper, Pat cries easily and is often driven to the catharsis of tears. But she never forgets whose she is. She recommends concentrating on this verse to help us remember our roots: "So do not fear, for I am with you; do not be dismayed, for I am your God. I will strengthen you and help you; I will uphold you with my righteous right hand" (Isaiah 41:10 NIV).

STAND FIRM

"The joy of the Lord is my strength," Pat claims. It is no show of phony spirituality. She means it. She has discovered what every believer ought to know: No matter what happens, the Lord is in control. Her steadfast confidence in Him in the midst of the storm blesses all who know her. She is a late afternoon survivor. No, make that a soarer.

Paul urged the Philippians to stand firm, "so that whether I come and see you or remain absent, I may hear of you that you are standing firm in one spirit, with one mind striving together for the faith of the gospel" (1:27). Paul's words evoke images of the Roman amphitheater. Ravenous beasts paced the cages, pawed the ground, ready to leap upon victims and rip them limb from limb. The Christians had no choice but to stand firm and meet the teeth and claws.

We, too, have no choice but to face the fiery darts of sorrow and suffering. We cannot run. Ephesians 6 mentions no spiritual armor for the back. And James instructs us, "Resist the devil and he will flee from you" (James 4:7). The instructions are to resist, not run away, no matter how rough it gets. Adopt the attitude of the French general who, upon discovering his army was surrounded, reportedly replied, "Wonderful! This means we can attack in any direction!"[5]

When we are tempted to give in during suffering, when we doubt God's goodness, we have one weapon to cling to. It is the "sword of the Spirit, which is the word of God" (Ephesians 6:17). Remembering His promises is the key to standing firm. Try the following prescriptions when you feel like caving in.

Illness	Prescription
Bitterness	Ephesians 4:31; James 3:14-16; Hebrews 12:14-15
Frustration	Proverbs 3:5-6; Matthew 11:28-30; 1 Samuel 26:3; 32:17

Uselessness	Jeremiah 18; Psalm 1; Jeremiah 17:7-8; 1 Corinthians 9:24-27
Doubt	Romans 8:38-39; 2 Timothy 1:12
Being Ridiculed	Philippians 2:3-4; Galatians 5:19-21
Being Patronized	1 Peter 5:5-6; Luke 18:9-14
Fear	Isaiah 41:10; 2 Timothy 1:7; 1 John 4:18; Proverbs 29:25

REALIZE WE ARE NOT ALONE

Because we are His, the Lord will allow some difficulty to befall us. He's gonna let it happen. Paul wrote, "For to you it has been granted for Christ's sake, not only to believe in Him, but also to suffer for His sake" (Philippians 1:29).

While it is certain that we will endure both the everyday and the extraordinary hassles of life, it is also certain that we will never be alone. Recognize this.

We are not alone because the Lord hurts when we hurt. Before the apostle Paul was blinded by the light of Christ on the Damascus road, he was determined to wipe out Christians. He held the coats of Stephen's murderers, but that wasn't enough. He wanted to quash the heresy. Although Paul couldn't possibly have injured Christ Himself, when Jesus stopped him cold on the way to Damascus, it was with these words: "Saul, Saul, why persecutest thou *me?*" (Acts 9:3-5 KJV, italics mine).

When Christians hurt, Christ hurts. Jesus feels every jab, every stone, every bitter accusation, unjust conviction, searing pain, wrenching loss that we do. We are not called to suffer alone.

Because we do not suffer alone, we can be assured that the Lord will see us through. God was with the three Hebrew men, Shadrach, Meshach, and Abed-nego, in the midst of the fiery furnace. God sent His angel to Daniel in the lions' den and to Peter in prison. He walked with Joseph on the sands of Egypt and spoke with Abraham when the patriarch had just about given up on being a daddy. He will be with you and me, too.

After Paul's conversion, the Lord sent Ananias to the apostle with these instructions: "Go, for he is a chosen instrument of Mine, to bear My name before the Gentiles and kings and the sons of Israel; for I will show him how much he must suffer for My name's sake" (Acts 9:15-16).

Job description number one for Paul was to suffer things for Jesus' sake. It's our job description, too.

CONSIDER IT ALL JOY

Challenging times can have perfect results in us, if we respond properly. In the words of James, "Consider it all joy, my brethren, when you encounter various trials, knowing that the testing of your faith produces endurance" (James 1:2-3). Paul said he rejoiced in suffering (Colossians 1:24). What was with these guys? Did they get their kicks out of being whipped up on?

No way. But they knew no one gets out of life alive. Tough times are coming. The best way to face them is with an attitude of joy. This does not mean, as some teach, that we are ecstatic because of the trials. We aren't called to plaster Cheshire cat smiles on our faces to conceal the pain. We don't have to grin and bear it, denying that it hurts. We can ask God "Why?" and tell our heavenly Father how much it aches. He knows, but it helps us to talk to Him about it.

The joy comes from the confidence that we have a Lord who is with us during trials, will see us through them, and will teach us a whole lot in the meantime. There is simple joy in knowing that nothing happens without the Father's permission, that everything happens with the purpose of making us more like Jesus, and that doses of reality are measured up by a loving hand which knows just what we need. Because of this we can live it up, lap it up, love it up, laugh it up, and refuse to let up till we find ourselves going up!

ASK HOW, NOT WHY

It is natural to ask, "Why?" when suffering engulfs. It is harder to ask of the Lord, "How?" How can I cooperate more fully to get maximum benefit? How does what is happening to me relate to what You desire to do in my life?

Charlie Jones writes in *Life Is Tremendous:*

The mark of a man who is growing is his understanding that things go wrong to make us more right. God never breaks a man down with problems except to build him up. The wild stallion may look beautiful on the mesa with his mane blowing in the wind, but he isn't much use until somebody breaks him so he can pull a load or carry a ride. Neither is a person much good until he is harnessed to teamwork and disciplined to guidance. God trains a man so the man can run free. That's an old law. You can fight it but you'll never change it. Imagine how superficial our lives would be if God didn't send circumstances that seemed disastrous for the moment but later prove enriching and meaningful.[6]

It is written of Christ himself that, "although He was a Son, He learned obedience from the things which He suffered" (Hebrews 5:8). In the words of the psalmist, "Before I was afflicted I went astray, but now I obey your word.... It was good for me to be afflicted so that I might learn your decrees" (Psalm 119:67,71 NIV).

Suffering matures and beautifies Christian character. Adoniram Judson was the son of a strict congregationalist minister and a poised, polished mother. A brilliant intellect, refined, cultured, proud, Judson mastered Greek by age twelve and entered the university at sixteen. A distinguished career as an orator or statesman lay before him. Then Judson met the Lord Jesus Christ as Savior at the age of twenty-one. His life radically changed as he dedicated himself to serving Christ.

Offered the pastorate of the largest church in Boston, Judson declined and, with his young wife, followed the call of God to India and Burma. It was six years before the Judsons saw their first Burmese convert. Within fourteen years, Mrs. Judson had died, as had each of their children. Adoniram could tell us of tortures, of being driven in chains across a blistering desert, of unjust imprisonments in filth-encrusted cells. He could tell us of smallpox epidemics and the agony of watching a beautiful young woman grow old and haggard before his eyes and before her time. He could tell us of the heart-wrenching deaths of his children.

He could tell us all of these things, but instead he would tell us of the love of Jesus. It was his favorite subject.

Before his death, Adoniram Judson had fulfilled two goals. He had translated the Bible into Burmese, and he presided over a native church of more than one hundred members. But at what cost! His words on sacrifice, service, and survival were these: "If I had not felt certain that every additional trial was ordered by infinite love and mercy, I could not have survived my accumulated sufferings."[7]

Oh that we could get to the place where no sacrifice would be too great for the cause of Christ! If we only could see every type of suffering as part and parcel of His larger, better plan!

THE THREE A'S

The Christian life is a battle. Satan the enemy, suffering the great leveler, God the sustainer. Want to be a contender in the last lap of life? At the risk of sounding crude or callous, be prepared to learn from what happens to you.

Paul exhorted young Timothy, "Fight the good fight of faith" (1 Timothy 6:12). Can we do less? When suffering strikes, I recommend the three A's to assist in fighting the good fight all the way home:

1. Acceptance. Realize suffering is coming. Accept it. Determine you'll take it no matter what, because you know your Father has allowed it for a reason.

2. Attitude. Know positively that because of the reputation and reliability of your heavenly Father, something good is going to result from your suffering.

3. Action. Anticipate the victory, but be sure to suit up. The coach always picks the best players to play the hardest quarters. This may be your finest hour.

DIGGING DEEPER

When we were kids, Mom made us take castor oil to get better and cod liver oil to stay better. I hated that stuff with a passion. It seemed like a lousy way to get better. Sometimes suffering seems like a lousy way to get better, too. But we don't have to understand everything that is going on in our lives. We do have to trust God in it.

We learn to live with need. We learn to live without the false concept of God as a great Daddy Warbucks in the sky waiting to shower us with goodies on demand.

Leonard and Sandy's adult son Marty was in a horrendous motorcycle accident months ago. He survived but is brain-damaged. The prognosis is dim. The joy is not. Finances drained, emotions frayed, Leonard said recently, "I guess we're just going to have to dig a little deeper."

Finishing his message before the Sanhedrin, Stephen looked up to behold the wonder of the glory of God as the heavens opened (Acts 7:55). Job's song of suffering was "Though He slay me, I will hope in Him" (Job 13:15). You, too, can see the glory through the gory. The crown through the crucible.

As our friend John Mackinnon neared physical death, he wrote eloquently about his thoughts and feelings. This meant he had to painstakingly peck out his messages on a computer keyboard as ALS ravaged his muscles and robbed him of coordination. I know no better way to close this chapter than with the perspective of one who hurt greatly and saw suffering as a higher way. It's interesting that John's early writings after his diagnosis center on the search for a cure and his confidence in God's will. But this farewell letter to his home church focuses on how the Father has used his illness. Read on and view the depth of a relationship with God made richer by suffering:

It is now well over a year since these circumstances of illness came upon me. But I want you to know, like the Apostle

Paul, these present circumstances have turned out for the greater progress of the gospel. Several close to me have come to life in the Light and others have deepened their faith in the Faithful One.

...But as my world has become smaller, His world has expanded. It is His world that excites me. Other than His people and His Word, He has helped me discover that I am not attached to anything in this world. It is His radiance that holds me captive. His arms my security. His paradise my home. Being part of His creation, my body groans eagerly for adoption as a son, the redemption of my body.

...He has deepened my understanding of what it means to be silent before Him. When we strive for duty, He usually desires devotion. When we seek Christian activity, He seeks intimacy. When we run our various programs, He may run us down. When we count the time, He counts the cost.

...So circle the wagons, put on your spiritual armor. The evil one will actively contest your devotional life. Give attention to building up the inner man. God doesn't use empty vessels on the front line.

...There is only one race. Run with endurance the race that is set before you, fixing your eyes on Jesus, the author and perfecter of faith. Run to win the prize. Press onward towards the goal for the prize of the upward call of God in Christ Jesus.[8]

It is with joy, unspeakable and full of glory, that John Mackinnon prepared to exit this life and enter eternity. The view from the top, as John would call his final days, was worth the climb.

REFLECTIONS

1. Accept the fact that suffering eventually goes with the territory.

2. Forge a plan to respond properly to your inevitable suffering.

3. Be sensitive to the losses your parents and older friends are encountering.

4. Learn now to trust God and see His goodness in the trials you face. This will prepare the way for tomorrow.

5. Recognize that pain is part of the process of turning things loose down here.

6. Keep an attitude of gratitude. Focus on what you have left, not on what you are losing.

CHAPTER 7

PLANNING FOR GRADUATION

CONFRONTING LIFE ONE DAY AT A TIME

🌢

I want to die in full stride, hopefully pursuing rather than being pursued.
The American Indian found it disgraceful to die in bed,
and we must not forget that death was
Patrick Henry's second choice.

WALTER M. BORTZ

I am not afraid of dying—I just don't want to be there when it happens.

WOODY ALLEN

How people cope with life-threatening circumstances runs the gamut. Refusing to accept one's own mortality seems the most prevalent. When such folks face the certainty of death, they are in denial and unprepared. The frequent comment is, "Now what do I do?"

Growing numbers of modern seniors are trying to find comfort in New Age thought and Eastern religion. The idea of reincarnation is becoming increasingly popular. If you go around more than once in life, then death is no big deal.

They are wrong. Death is a big deal.

Cowboy poet Wallace McRae of Forsyth, Montana, penned a hilarious piece on the truth about reincarnation. One of my favorites, it is already considered a classic. Here is Slim's philosophy lesson, just for grins:

REINCARNATION
by Wallace McRae

"What does reincarnation mean?"
A cowpoke ast his friend.
His pal replied, "It happens when
Yer life has reached its end.
They comb yer hair, and warsh yer neck,
And clean yer fingernails,
And lay you in a padded box
Away from life's travails.

"The box and you goes in a hole,
That's been dug into the ground.
Reincarnation starts in when
You're planted 'neath a mound.
Them clods melt down, just like yer box,
And you who is inside.
And then yore just beginnin' on
Yer transformation ride.

"In a while the grass'll grow
Upon yer rendered mound.
Till some day on yer moldered grave
A lonely flower is found.
And say a hoss should wander by
And graze upon this flower

That once wuz you, but now's become
Yer vegetative bower.

"The posey that the hoss done ate
Up, with his other feed,
Makes bone, and fat, and muscle
Essential to the steed.
But some is left that he can't use
And so it passes through,
And finally lays upon the ground.
This thing, that once wuz you.

"Then say, by chance, I wanders by
And sees this upon the ground,
And I ponders, and I wonders at,
The object that I found.
I thinks of reincarnation,
Of life, and death, and such,
And come away concludin': Slim,
You ain't changed all that much."[1]

GRADUATION DAY

For the Christian, death is a departure to meet someone you have longed to see all through life. It isn't often you get to meet someone who loves you so much He would rather die than live without you!

When my father succumbed to cancer eight years ago, the lady helping with the music at the memorial service said that Dad had graduated and that we were here to help him celebrate his graduation. She was right; that we did.

Graduation day. Often we think of a graduation as the end of a certain phase of life, which it is. Yet the word *commencement* means beginning. We commence a new life after graduation. We are promoted—after high school to college or other training, after college to career.

And after life, we are promoted to afterlife. This ultimate graduation day comes for us all.

WHEN GRADUATION COMES TOO EARLY

The problem is, some of us check out sooner than expected. Jack and Jean attended church every Sunday. Jean was a pastor's dream. She was active in the women's ministries, sent cards to shut-ins, and made regular hospital visits. Jack was quiet but always wore a pleasant smile. He had a diabetic flare-up and was down for a while, but everything seemed normal.

Early one morning Jack told Jean he was going fishing. Several hours later his empty boat was found floating on the lake. A couple days later, divers discovered his body at the bottom. He had evidently tied weights to his ankles and jumped overboard.

Jack was another senior suicide. Like so many despondent in their later years, he gave up on life. It was later revealed that a diabetic depression linked with extended family problems probably drove him over the edge.

Although Jack's methods were unusual, his intentions and their tragic result, were not. Minirth, Meier, and Reed state that one of the major mental problems among seniors is depression, the "single most common psychological disorder in this age group." This depression, according to the doctors, is sometimes openly evident in facial expressions and hopeless thinking.

More subtly and insidiously, it emerges in a masked form with such symptoms as sleep disturbances, health worries, appetite loss, energy decrease, back pain, and abnormal concern about bodily functions.

Suicide is not an uncommon end result. *Thirty percent of all self-inflicted deaths occur among those who are sixty-five and older.* Often the victim is alone, in poor health, desiring to escape.[2] The lethal combination seems to be deteriorating health, lack of purpose, and poor interpersonal relationships.

UNNECESSARY LOSSES

Why do many seniors choose to end life rather than live life? Charles Sell recounts the story of an old man who left a suicide note before taking his life. The note simply read, "I lost my hat today; after losing so much, that was one more loss than I could handle."[3] The story illustrates a universal truth: Often the losses of aging are more than we want to endure.

One cannot deny that aging is accompanied by loss. Loss of hair, teeth, eyesight, hearing, muscle tone. Loss of family, friends, work. Loss of skills and abilities. You may not be the tennis player you once were. You won't have the reflexes to race Indy cars. Your seniors aerobics class will start to remind you of your favorite breakfast cereal: snap, crackle, and pop!

Solomon described aging metaphorically in Ecclesiastes 12 as a time when, among other things, "the grinders [teeth] cease because they are few" and the eyes, "those looking through the windows grow dim" (verse 3 NIV). Solomon understood what it was to grow old.

Aging is probably best described as shaking like a Ford fender, the whole while wondering what's going to fall off next.

As Lloyd Cory says, "People often ask, 'What's new?' I've come to that stage in life when if anything's new it's apt to be a symptom."[4] Either that, or it's something they just put in.

I'll always remember when my father and mother realized that they couldn't do everything they used to do. For years it had been a joint labor to get a steer they had raised into their high-backed pickup truck to be conveyed to the slaughterhouse. My apologies to vegetarians and animal rights activists, but Mom and Dad even named the future hamburger and took great delight in announcing, "We're eating Sonny!"

On their last solo trip to market, the large, frisky steer must have figured out their intentions. He nearly kicked out the tailgate, and Dad almost drove off the road into a ditch. Calming Dad and the steer was no easy task. My folks admitted they were just getting too old for all this. They laughed, but having to concede they would need help on market day was a little tough. It was just one more small loss—insignificant in and of itself, but a sign that they were growing older and eventually would need other kinds of assistance.

It was much harder when Dad had to give up driving, sell the family home, quit planting a garden large enough to feed the whole block, and move into a retirement home. The physical problems he had suffered most of his life began to accumulate, and he needed additional rest and sedation just to keep going. I'll always remember saying goodbye that August morning, knowing in my heart that it would be the last time. He mustered enough strength to make his famous pies, fudge, and divinity for the holidays. Early that spring his family gathered to celebrate his graduation.

I don't think Dad ever considered taking his own life, but many seniors do. And many succeed—like Jim, a friend for years who had done tremendous things during his life to serve kids and families as a Christian camp director. Something cracked one day, and Jim was gone.

Two men from church, both diagnosed with cancer, took their lives within a week of each other. All of these tragic ends were unnecessary losses—premature stops in the race of life.

One of the things you admire most about Job in the Old Testament is that although everything in his life fell apart and the wagon turned over, he never once talked about taking his own life.

WHAT IS A DIGNIFIED DEATH?

Certain types of suicide are actually receiving positive press these days.

Advice columnist Ann Landers recently devoted two days to printing the responses of readers to a letter from a man who had signed himself, "85 and Waiting." Fearing the ravages of old age as he visited nursing-home-bound friends in various degrees of incapacitation, "85" expressed his hope that one day people would be allowed to exit life painlessly and with dignity. Responses to "85 and Waiting" flooded Ann's mailroom and included the following:

From Lancaster, Pennsylvania: Thank you for your courageous stand on an individual's right to die. My brother was diagnosed HIV positive 10 years ago. When his disease became truly debilitating, he discussed with me his plan to "exit gracefully." He chose the time, took an overdose of sleeping pills, went to sleep and never woke up. Not only did he spare himself a lot of agony and pain, we were spared as well.

From Springfield, Virginia: Following a stroke, my father lived for two years in a nursing home. My mother is now in a "health care center." She has been there for five years. Her monthly care bill is $2,700. Her savings are just about gone. She is distressed because the inheritance she planned for her grandchildren is slipping away.

From Panama City, Florida: My mother has been languishing in a nursing home for five years. The nursing staff is constantly fighting her bed sores, but she is literally rotting away. This is not happening to me. I will see to it well ahead of time.

From Syracuse, New York: Until the medical community realizes that death is not a doctor's failure but an inevitable end for us all, we will, unfortunately, continue to torture our sick and our elderly.[5]

On a more ominous note, disability advocate Katie Letcher Lyle penned an opinion piece for *Newsweek* magazine in which she argues the gentle mercy killing of her pet cat provides a pattern suitable for society to emulate. Lyle specifically mentions the benefits that would result from euthanizing a "beloved, ancient friend, her mind absolutely gone for six years, her body ticking on relentlessly." How tragic that we cannot give Fritchie the "swift, merciful death we gave our pet," mourns

Lyle. Shockingly, Lyle even suggests that the euthanization of a violent, mentally retarded yet physically healthy man named Henry would be a merciful solution to the problem of his tormented existence as well.[6]

Lyle's position seems extreme today. But is it a sign of the future? Kerby Anderson observes:

> For centuries Western culture in general and Christians in particular have believed in the sanctity of human life. Unfortunately, this view is beginning to erode into a "quality of life" standard. Before, the disabled, retarded, and infirm were seen as having a special place in God's world; but today medical personnel judge a person's fitness for life on the basis of a perceived quality of life or lack of such quality.
>
> No longer is life seen as sacred and worthy of being saved.[7]

In late twentieth century America, some suicides and assisted deaths are increasingly deemed okay by society. Folks who are terminally ill, in vegetative states, suffering horrendous pain, slipping into irreversible dementias, are thought by many people to have the right to end it all or to have it ended for them. Even extreme old age is sometimes seen as a reason to die, not an accomplishment to celebrate.

When the financial, emotional, and physical pressures of a debilitating condition become too great for family or patient, it is often culturally acceptable to call it quits on life. We are even giving permission for family members to make such decisions for comatose or mentally incompetent loved ones. We've come up with politically correct euphemisms for these actions. Deathspeak.

Disability advocate Joni Eareckson Tada, in her excellent treatment of the subject, *When Is It Right to Die?*, lists the following definitions (paraphrased below) under the broad heading "Euthanasia":

Voluntary euthanasia—causing death with the person's consent and approval

Nonvoluntary euthanasia—in the event of the patient's incompetence, causing death without the person's consent through the approval of family members, doctors, or the courts

Involuntary euthanasia—causing the death of a person against his will no matter the circumstances

Death selection—systematic, involuntary euthanasia against people whose lives are no longer considered socially useful

Active euthanasia—mercy killing in which action is taken to cause another's death

Passive euthanasia—mercy killing by withholding or withdrawing food, water, or medical treatment

Assisted suicide—when a physician or other individual aids a person toward death.[8]

These terms are bandied about in our courts, hospitals, newspapers, magazines, medical journals, and ethics classes. Our culture is demanding we make certain choices.

As Christians we must not bow to societal pressures without examining issues in the light of Scripture. We must ask ourselves: Is it ever okay to give up on life? To pull the trigger? To pull the plug? Is it ever okay to refuse medical treatment? To kill ourselves? To allow ourselves to die? To allow a loved one to die? What does the Bible say? What should be our theology of death and the dying process?

As you read this, it may be easier for you to answer such questions about some situations than others. It may make perfect sense to say about someone who is depressed, "No, he shouldn't take the 'easy' way out!" But for someone who is suffering the horrors of AIDS, the ravages of a painful, terminal cancer, the mental suffocation of senile dementia, you might just think death would be a blessing. He's going to die anyway. Why not accelerate the process and decelerate the suffering? Why not make it easier on everyone?

Do we ever, truly, have the "right to die"?

Joni Eareckson Tada points out that the phrase "right to die" is deceptive and illogical. Death is not a right; it is an inevitability. We will all die.[9] One of our local doctors says death is merely the anaesthetic God uses while He is changing our bodies. Let us, then, rephrase our question: Do we have the right to accelerate death?

Time, space, and the emphasis of this book permit us to examine these issues only from the perspective of the senior years. For a broader analysis of the ethics of "right to die" philosophies, I refer you to Tada's *When Is It Right to Die?*,

C. Everett Koop's *Whatever Happened to the Human Race?*, and Kerby Anderson's *Living Ethically in the 90s*. Tada, a quadriplegic, offers an especially compelling perspective on the subject.

It's also helpful to examine how clearly the apostle Paul spoke to this question in his letter to the Philippians.

DEATH BENEFITS: WAS PAUL AFRAID TO DIE?

When writing Philippians, the apostle Paul faced the possibility of imminent death. Talk about depressing! His fate hinged on the unpredictable behavior of a psychopath, Nero, who at any moment might choose to call up Paul's number as lion food for the Colosseum.

Not only that, but from Scripture we know that Paul suffered some type of infirmity—a "thorn in the flesh," as he called it. We read in 2 Corinthians 12:7-9 that Paul had prayed to ask the Lord to remove this thorn, but the Lord had answered, "My grace is sufficient for you, for my power is made perfect in weakness." Perhaps this thorn was poor eyesight (Galatians 6:11). Maybe being visually impaired was only one of the apostle's handicaps. We know from his writings that he had suffered intense physical abuse since becoming a Christian. We can't imagine how many systems Paul had to check on before he could crank it up in the morning. Bruised and bloodied, he still wrote in 2 Corinthians 4:9, "We are persecuted, but are never deserted: we may be knocked down but we are never knocked out" (Phillips).

If there was ever a guy who had an excuse for grabbing the meat wagon before the marathon was done, it was Paul. His entire Christian life seems to have run precariously close to the ditch. Second Corinthians 1:8-11 tells of just such an experience.

We don't know what the situation was, but difficulties became so intense at one of the pit stops that Paul and Timothy thought they would be forced from the race. Thank God they weren't. And then came prison!

Paul's life was restricted, uncomfortable, dependent upon the physical aid and financial assistance of others. He was hamstrung and hurting, but you would have never known it to talk to him.

Surely at times death seemed preferable to continuing with the struggle of life. In the words of the apostle: "For to me, to live is Christ, and to die is gain. But if I am to live on in the flesh, this will mean fruitful labor for me; and I do not know which to choose. But I am hard pressed from both directions, having the desire to depart and be with Christ, for that is very much better; yet to remain on in the flesh is more necessary for your sake" (Philippians 1:21-24).

Notice, for Paul, living was Christ and dying was gain. Death held only fascination for him. He knew that to be absent from the body was to be present with the Lord (2 Corinthians 5:8). He lived for Christ down here; death would only mean gaining more of Christ. As the Spirit revealed to the apostle John in the book of Revelation, "Blessed are the dead who die in the Lord from now on" (14:13).

Unlike Paul, we may find death a fearful thing. It is an unknown realm, an untried quantity. It may come with a great deal of pain. It may take its toll on our family's emotions, strength, and finances. It may rob us of our minds, gnaw away at our bodies, rub raw our emotions. It may come inexorably slowly. There are no guarantees we'll go quietly and in our sleep.

Only a fool would claim the dying process has no disadvantages. But only a fool would overlook the fact that death also has advantages for the Christian. Paul understood his death benefits.

Episcopal bishop Warren Chandler said when facing his own demise, "My Father owns the land on both sides of the river. Why should I fear?"[10] When death comes, the believer has this to hang on to: Jesus Christ has been there. The cry from the cross, "It is finished," was the trumpet fanfare at the gate of eternity. There Jesus crossed the river and accepted the punishment, separation from God, that we as sinners deserve. From death's murky depths He arose again three days later. He had the last word.

To Paul, death was appealing, as it is to many seniors when life becomes simply too arduous a battle to continue. We get tired of running uphill into the wind.

Death, for the Christian, is better than life. Paul knew he would be gaining more of Christ. He would also be cashing in on all his benefits and investments. These eternal rewards for right-motivated Christian service in life are mentioned by Paul in his farewell address to young Timothy: "In the future there is laid up for me the crown of righteousness, which the Lord, the righteous Judge, will award to me on that day; and not only to me, but also to all who have loved His appearing" (2 Timothy 4:8).

Paul was not afraid to die. But despite his limitations and infirmities, neither was he afraid to live. Finishing was important to him. Breaking the tape and falling into your Father's arms is the way to go.

SAY YES TO LIFE

The Greek word translated "depart" in Philippians 1:23 conveys the idea of hoisting anchor and setting off to sea, or of folding up a tent and going home. Earthly life is not forever. This is not all there is. Contrary to all the beer commercials, it does get a whole lot better than this.

Paul was fully ready to be with Christ. But he was also ready to say yes to life. "To remain on in the flesh is more necessary for your sake," wrote Paul. His work was not finished. Occasions for fruitful labor remained.

So what does this mean to us? No matter how tough it gets, there are still occasions for fruitful labor as long as the Lord allows us to live. Jesus said, "By this is My Father glorified, that you bear much fruit" (John 15:8).

People listen to folks who are going through it. When you can say, "I've been there," you have earned the right to be heard. The way you exit and the words you use could do more for the kingdom than all your previous ministry. It does matter to the Father how we finish.

It should encourage those of us in the final laps of life to know that lasting fruit is borne more by what we are than by what we do or say. No matter how old, weak, or sick we are, we can still magnify the Lord. We can still influence our children and grandchildren. We can still be a beacon to the lost and lonely by reaching out instead of keeping to ourselves. We can let others see Christ living in us and carrying us through the valley. We can show people that we have surrendered to the sovereignty of God and that He is good.

The way I want to go out is described in Paul's farewell message in 2 Timothy 4:6-8. I want to recognize in the present that the time of my departure is at hand (verse 6). As for the past, I want to say that I fought the good fight, finished the course, kept the faith (verse 7). And I want to look ahead to the future and the crown of righteousness awaiting me in eternity (verse 8).

For the believer, death is good. Don't be afraid to die, but die in God's time, not yours. Until you die, live. You have work to do and fruit to bear. Do nothing to artificially accelerate the inevitable. When life is at its toughest, God may be doing his greatest work in and through you.

WHEN LIFE SEEMS UNFRUITFUL

No discussion of the biblical ethics of life and death among seniors would be complete without examining a hard question. What about lives that seem completely fruitless, unproductive, meaningless? Many of us have seen loved ones live out just this sort of existence. Irreversible illness. Brain damage. Alzheimer's disease. Cancer. Pain. Sometimes isn't it merciful to allow someone to die? To give them a pleasant shove toward everlasting life?

Biblically, the answer is no. It is never our prerogative to interfere with the Father's plans. He reigns! He does all things well. God uses suffering, even seemingly senseless suffering, to His glory. Ours is not to choose the means of exit, but to ask for strength for the struggle.

There is a spiritual warfare we cannot see. Who knows what goes on in the spirit of a comatose or incoherent person? Jean is suffering the final stages of Alzheimer's disease, yet tears roll down her face when favorite hymns are played. She cannot talk, seemingly cannot recognize loved ones, but God's Spirit in her responds to the music of the soul. Who can say what supernatural battles are waged in the spiritual realm? Who can measure the impact of the witness of her godly husband and family in the face of all this?

There is also the issue of the sanctity of life. Life is a sacred gift from the Father's hand. Ours is the stewardship of that life. Life, all human life, has inherent value.

When God seems slow, it is ours to wait until He calls. The prophet Elijah sat by a dry brook. The temptation to provide for himself was real. But Elijah waited till the word of the Lord came, telling him to head to Zarephath. The result? Plenty of food. King Saul forced the issue and performed a sacrifice instead of waiting for Samuel to do it God's way. The result? Disaster.

In matters of life and death, it is best to wait and watch God work.

THE DIFFERENCE BETWEEN DYING AND DEATH

"It is appointed for men to die once and after this comes judgment" (Hebrews 9:27). There will be a time for each of us where death is unavoidable. Then we will be in the process of dying. At this juncture, extraordinary medical measures do not prolong life, they prolong death.

For questions of ethics related to the heroic medical treatment of your family members, I again refer you to Joni Eareckson Tada's book. It is excellent, written from a perspective few of us have but, as C. Everett Koop accurately states in the foreword, many will share after reading. Deciding not to prolong your death or the death of your loved one is different from assisting or hastening that death. There are many factors involved, too many to do justice here. I urge you to examine the issues and reach your conclusions before you must make decisions of life and death. You don't want to be talked into or out of critical choices concerning your loved ones when you are under terrific stress or dealing with overwhelming grief.

FINAL SOLUTION

To date, retired Michigan pathologist Dr. Jack Kevorkian has reportedly assisted over twenty patients to commit suicide. Kevorkian reportedly intends to go out this way himself some day. So far his clients have included individuals not necessarily suffering terminal illnesses, but debilitating conditions for whom life is too difficult, arduous, costly, frustrating, humiliating, financially draining, painful. From cancer to M.S. to Alzheimer's, what all Kevorkian's suicide clients have had in common is that they opted out of life when it became too tough.

Life couldn't have been much tougher than it was for Paul O'Brien. Diagnosed several years ago with a degenerative, inoperable heart condition, such simple feats as walking up a few stairs became impossible for Paul. Early retirement became a necessity. His wife, Irene, a gifted writer, chronicles their decision for life:

> Four years ago, Paul and I deliberately decided life is for the living. For us to live in fear of how or where we will die destroys how we will live....
>
> On occasion, at day's end, I helped Paul into bed, gave him a "little white pill," and sat quietly by his side until his breathing returned to normal. And, yes, sometimes the unknown wells up inside, pours out in tears, and sets a stone in the pit of my stomach. But those feelings are not worthy of our Savior's love. In those moments I recall David's words, "For I cried unto the Lord and He answered me. He freed me from all my fears" (Psalm 34:4).

An aged philosopher, Horace Kallen, said it perfectly. "There are persons who shape their lives by the fear of death, and persons who shape their lives by the joy and satisfaction of life.... Whenever it [death] comes, I intend to die living.[11]

A few years after his heart condition was diagnosed, Paul and Irene O'Brien received more bad news: a cancer which had invaded Paul's body would certainly kill him. His earthly journey came to an end within a year.

But his end was peaceful. He had every reason to give in early, but he hung on till one pre-dawn morning when he roused himself for a final trip to the living room. There his struggle ceased, in God's time. "Because of his attitude," writes Irene, "I was able to cope with his illness. He never complained and never made demands (I didn't know I was a care giver until somebody pointed it out to me after he was gone). When asked how he was, he was always, 'Great,' or 'Tough.' His sense of humor never left him."

It would have been easy for Paul O'Brien to opt out of life in any of the years when breathing was arduous and exertion impossible. He certainly had an excuse when his body was riddled with cancer. But he chose life to its fullest, and his final years were fruitful. A bride of twenty-one years, twelve children and step-children, and seventeen grandchildren remember well his courage and faith.

REFLECTIONS

1. A man who aims at nothing usually hits it. If you are in mid-life, develop a plan for the next fifteen years of your life.

2. Accept your own mortality. Live each day in view of it. This philosophy will affect how you relate to your family and friends.

3. Open a discussion with your parents about their wishes concerning life support and heroic, life-saving measures. Have this same talk with your spouse. Make the tough decisions now, before you need to make them.

4. Record on tape or in writing a statement of your salvation experience to leave as a legacy for friends and family.

5. If you are a senior, accept the fact you are in the last quarter of life and give it all you've got.

6. Update your will, and make plans and arrangements for your departure so it will be easier on your family. Explain your desires about the use of medical technology to sustain your life or prolong your death. Investigate and make the tough decisions now.

CHAPTER 8

THE MIND OF CHRIST

SELFISHNESS OR SERVANTHOOD?

☞

*I have more trouble with D. L. Moody
than with any other man I ever met.*

DWIGHT L. MOODY

Everyone around the church said, "Let George do it," and he did it. The board would vote on Sunday, and by Monday George was working on what they had approved. It pleased George so much to be able to help, and it brought such joy to the body of believers. On his graduation day, George was hip-deep in a church remodeling project. He came home for a break and shortly thereafter showed up in glory.

I miss him still, but his love of the Lord and commitment to serve made his funeral easy to preach. Everyone laughed in agreement when I said that George had probably already located his wife Elizabeth's mansion in heaven and was in the process of re-doing the cabinets. He was that kind of guy. Humble. Willing to do anything. Putting others first. He finished well.

Not so with old man Coot (you guessed it—not his real name). He cloistered himself at home with his wife. You seldom saw him in the yard unless he was yelling at the neighbor kids who trespassed on his property to retrieve their basketball. His social life was nil. You got the feeling he was waiting for the call up yonder and that the Lord was delaying, too, because He didn't know what He was going to do with him when he got there.

One fellow was a real servant, the other, real selfish.

REAL LIFE

A great part of our march toward maturity involves learning to find our place in life, a place where we are secure and comfortable under authority. We discover in the process that much of real life is doing what you have to do.

As children we follow the direction of parents. As teens we are under the authority of teachers, coaches, and parents. Young adulthood brings professors and bosses. In our twenties and thirties we acquire a spouse, a set of in-laws, and a mortgage. Now we've got a whole new ball game.

Child-rearing consumes most of our time for the next couple decades. I remember a silly song about a guy named Charlie and the M.T.A. Charlie couldn't get off that train and his wife would throw him a sandwich whenever the train came rumblin' through. I felt like that's what I did for Pearl as she drove and drove our five children to school events, swim meets, endless practices and activities.

Then comes college. Try paying for five higher educations on a minister's salary. And our youngest tried graduate school! We invented novel ways to stretch the budget. Tube steaks and gourmet guess-whats got us a long way down the road. Eating out was out, so we let the kids help with the cooking till the day our German shepherd got sick from the leftovers.

Ah, but when the kids are all raised, the pets have all died, the mortgage is (almost) paid off, then, finally, our culture says life begins. We can shut her down and do what we want. The whistle blows and the long day's work is finally done.

"We stayed home twenty years. First, the children were too small, then too busy with school. Then we were paying for their school and couldn't afford to go anywhere. Now it's our turn!" exclaimed Helen on a rare rest stop at home between trips to Europe and the Far East. She and her husband plan to see and do it all. Retirement will be *their* time.

Helen has a point. Humans are geared to need rest and recreation. Pearl and I are avid believers in T. S. Eliot's philosophy of life: "Most of us can only bear so much reality." As Vance Havner put it, "If you don't come apart and rest awhile, you will come apart." A cycle of work-renewal-work-renewal is scriptural.

Longer periods of rest refresh us, too. Weekends away revive marriages. Vacations are great for building family ties—some of our very best family memories are of camping trips with our kids.

The senior years provide an ideal time to plan to get away from it all. If you are financially able, it is a fabulous occasion for the trip you've always wanted to take. Or if your health allows, you might take up the sport or activity you've thought about. Don't be afraid to have fun! R & R is good for us at all ages.

But let me warn you, R & R as a lifestyle will ultimately be unfulfilling for the Christian. It may even kill you! You were made for more. Our lives demand balance.

THE CONFLICT OF THE OLD AND NEW

Pleasure is addictive. It always takes more to achieve the same result. Couples in the retirement communities where we ministered would sometimes return from extravagant vacations and fall into six-month funks of depression, literally. They wanted more.

Seniors dissatisfied with hedonistic retirement discover what nobody told them: A lifestyle of self-indulgence and spending money cannot bring the satisfaction which comes from spending ourselves. We were made in the image of God, and among other things, that means we need to think beyond ourselves. We long for significance—to be thought of graciously and remembered generously. We want to make a difference. We simply feel better when we give of ourselves in a meaningful way.

Reporting on the results of interviews with 623 persons, Lisle Marbury Goodman concluded that the more complete one's life is in terms of the fulfillment of one's destiny and creative capacities, the less one fears death. People fear the incompleteness of their lives more than death. According to Paul B. Maves, this means, "Persons need to be involved in life projects that have significance."[1]

The issue is selfishness versus servanthood. In that conflict we Christians find ourselves at war with ourselves. What Scripture calls the old nature, what we were before coming to Christ, is essentially selfish. When we become believers, a new nature dwells within us, coexisting with the old. We now have an inclination to do God's will. Within us also is the Holy Spirit, and it is He who energizes our new nature to right action. We do not lose the old nature until we die. Every day, every hour, every minute we face a choice: Will we submit to the old nature or be ruled by the new? As Keith L. Brooks aptly puts it, "Insofar as we yield to him, the mind of the Master will become the master of our minds."[2]

Christian life is always a conflict between two natures. The one we feed dominates. Paul wrote of his own struggle with these natures: "For that which I am doing, I do not understand; for I am not practicing what I would like to do, but I am doing the very thing I hate" (Romans 7:15).

The old nature is selfish. It seeks its own. It doubts, fears, is anxious, bitter, and materialistic. It wrongly interprets the actions and motives of others. It displays itself in hostility, guilt, depression, and insecurity. In senior adulthood, it comes out in the critical, unforgiving heart. Satan can really do a number when he finds a believer living in the old nature. It is ugly, ugly, ugly! The arrogant, unbending senior is Satan's masterpiece.

The new nature is just the opposite. It is humble. It trusts God even when circumstances dictate trust is foolish. It is thankful, positive, anticipating ultimate victory. It looks beyond present trouble to a greater purpose. The new mind manifests itself by "taking every thought captive to the obedience of Christ" (2 Corinthians 10:5). The new nature serves unselfishly, willingly, until all earthly life is gone.

It is perhaps when thinking of this new, divine nature within us that Paul urged his readers at Philippi: "Do nothing from selfishness or empty conceit, but with humility of mind regard one another as better than yourselves" (2:3-4). And that brings us to our next goal: Put others first! To put it succinctly, we are to display the mind of Christ (2:5).

THE MIND OF CHRIST

What is this mind of Christ?

The mind of Christ is humble, seeking to serve rather than to be served (Mark 10:45). It is the new nature in the driver's seat with the old locked in the trunk. Jesus personified the new nature so we could see a flesh and blood example of perfect goodness and selflessness. He showed us how the mind of God operates. In his letter to the Philippians, Paul mentioned three ways Christ did this:

> Jesus let go.
> Jesus emptied himself.
> Jesus sacrificed himself to serve.

Christ, "although He existed in the form of God, did not regard equality with God a thing to be grasped" (2:6). The word "grasped" may also be translated "grasped eagerly." It means to clutch, to cling to. The Son of God did not maintain a hammerlock on His position in heaven but laid aside everything to serve us. He let go.

Jesus' life was a progressive letting go. He traded the honor of heaven for the hovels of earth. "For you know the grace of our Lord Jesus Christ, that though He was rich, yet for your sake He became poor, that you through His poverty might become rich" (2 Corinthians 8:9).

Jesus borrowed a place to be born, a house to sleep in, a boat to preach from, an animal to ride upon, a tomb to be buried in. At the cross He relinquished His mother to the care of another. For three hours one Friday afternoon He let go of the Father to experience the isolation of separation from God, becoming sin for us so that we need never know that awful aloneness.

In this letting go, Jesus "emptied Himself," Paul explained, "taking the form of a bondservant, and being made in the likeness of men" (Philippians 2:7). When He entered the human race, Jesus did not stop being God. He simply stripped Himself of the prerogatives of His true rank to walk among us.

At the moment he divested himself of the apparel of the Son, Christ took on the apron of the servant. He leaped into the world of humanity, split time with His coming, and accomplished our redemption with His exit. Healing the sick, restoring sight to the blind, calming the grief-stricken, raising the dead, feeding the hungry, wiping the feet of the disciples, going to the cross...in all and through all, Jesus served (Matthew 20:26-28). The writer of the book of Hebrews put it this way: "But we do see Him who has been made for a little while lower than the angels, namely, Jesus, because of the suffering of death crowned with glory and honor, that by the grace of God He might taste death for every one" (2:9).

This is His mind. "Father, if it be possible, let this cup pass from Me," Jesus humbly asked in the garden of Gethsemane before His arrest. "Nevertheless, not My will but Yours be done!" (Matthew 26:39). Christ was obedient to death—even the death of the cross. He chose servanthood over selfishness and in all humility made the supreme sacrifice.

CHANGING YOUR MIND

Senior adulthood is, for most of us, a time of letting go, of emptying, of choices. Retirement experts observe that we must detach from the old career, the old life, in order to be fruitful in the new.[3] We let go of the past. We choose what to empha-size in the future.

In the same way, as we become detached from the old nature and submissive to the new nature, we see in retirement possibilities for service. Culturally we've got a good start on humility already, for seniors are seen as lowly by many younger people. Why not accept the changes graciously and pour our-selves into service for God? We might be amazed at the results.

The American Association of Retired Persons listed "service to others" as one of twelve areas to be considered while plan-ning for retirement.[4] Jerry White calls retired Christians the "greatest untapped missionary and spiritual work force in the United States."[5] And so we are.

A picture hanging in our home states, "Ministry doesn't pay much but the retirement benefits are out of this world."

Jesus went the distance at Calvary for us. Can we do less for Him in our latter years when soon we shall see Him face to face?

THREE KEY PLAYERS

Paul. Real winners are part of a team. Paul understood that. In his words, he was "being poured out as a drink offering upon the sacrifice and service of your faith" (Philippians 2:17). This drink offering was a cup of wine poured upon a burnt offering in the Jewish sacrificial system. Like the Lord Jesus, Paul was willing to be spilled out. If he were completely spent in service to others for Jesus, he would only "rejoice" (2:17). He was run-ning all out for the finish line: "But I do not consider my life of any account as dear to myself, in order that I may finish my course and the ministry which I received from the Lord Jesus, to testify solemnly of the gospel of the grace of God" (Acts 20:24).

The finish line is not retirement. It is physical death, or the day of Christ mentioned by Paul in Philippians 1:6 and 2:16. According to Scripture, there will be a time of reward for those of us who have trusted Christ as Savior.

How we have spent our time will be a consideration when we appear before Christ. We don't have the time to blow smoke and waste precious days in selfish pursuits when we could be serving Jesus. Selfishness diminishes us. Servanthood exalts.

Jesus was a finisher. So was Paul. Death didn't scare him. He counted the cost and chose to throw himself perpetually on the line for Christ. There was nothing too difficult, no sacrifice too big. He could echo the words of John: "We know love by this, that He laid down His life for us; and we ought to lay down our lives for the brethren" (1 John 3:6).

Paul rejoiced in his personal sacrifice. Why not? The race run well is reason for rejoicing.

Timothy. The mind of Christ is sacrifice and servanthood. Paul lived it. So did his young protégé Timothy.

Although his real dad was Greek, Timothy had been raised by his godly Jewish grandmother and mother, Lois and Eunice. Timothy adopted Paul as a surrogate father when the apostle came to Lystra. Paul loved Timothy as a son and wrote him the last of his known letters, what we call 2 Timothy.

Timothy was a "kindred spirit" (2:20). Paul was glad to send him to the Philippians. There was no one else who would be as genuinely concerned for their welfare. No one as faithful. No one as loving. No one as service-minded. Timothy would go anywhere, do anything, at any cost, for Jesus and other believers.

Were we to meet Timothy today, we would know instantly how much he cared for others. His face would speak compassion.

His gentle speech would reveal sensitivity. His actions would say availability.

Another man, when asked to go to Philippi to check on the believers, might have thought, "No way. I've got too much to do. Let them handle their own problems. That's Paul's church, not mine." As Paul reported of the others, "They all seek after their own interests, not those of Christ Jesus" (2:21).

What consumes us? Where do our passions lie? The answer may have more to do with money, material things, power, position, or pleasure than with the Lord Jesus. Even good things like family, health, and our future can excessively preoccupy us.

I'd venture to say that the vast majority of people, including Christians, seek their own things and not the things of Christ. *I* is their god; *self* is their goal; *me, me, me,* their slogan.

Not Timothy. He was willing to go the extra mile, spend the extra dollar, stay the extra hour. We need more like him. "Your care for others is a measure of your greatness" (Luke 9:48 TLB). With compassion and commitment to Christ, Paul and Timothy were great men.

Epaphroditus. There was another hall of famer from Philippi. Paul's second living object lesson of Christ-mindedness is Epaphroditus.

Lots of us love work. We can lie beside it all day. But you'd never catch Epaphroditus taking an extra coffee break in the work of Christ. His name meant "charming," and he must have been. He was special. Paul called him a "fellow soldier," "fellow worker," and "brother"—high praise from the apostle who was never given to flattery.

Epaphroditus was the only person in Philippi willing to convey the congregation's love offering to Paul in Rome.

Evidently, Epaphroditus rearranged his affairs in order to take such a long journey. He may have taken a sabbatical from work. Or maybe he was in the process of handing over the family business to his sons and grandsons.

Whatever inconvenience it caused, Epaphroditus didn't care. He knew what was important. What was eternal. When work for the kingdom of God needed to be done, Epaphroditus didn't just sit down till the feeling went away. He plunged in, using his freedom from the traditional methods of earning a living to give of himself.

To do this, Epaphroditus had to endure a six-hundred-mile journey that involved crossing Macedonia, sailing the Adriatic Sea, then journeying across much of Italy to Rome. A twenty-mile-per-day pace, unrealistically fast, would have meant a thirty-day trip in the very best of conditions. Epaphroditus must have been exhausted when he reached Paul.

It doesn't take much to imagine that Epaphroditus had a part in the explosion of the gospel taking place in Rome because of Paul's imprisonment. There were military families, soldiers, government officials, and common folks to be contacted. Follow-up visits to new converts had to be made. Thousands of questions had to be answered. In prison, Paul could only handle a fraction of what had to be done. So Epaphroditus was needed. He was not a man who excused himself from hard work. He chose to serve, and he nearly died in the process.

The long journey, lack of sleep, constant work in Rome, all combined to make Epaphroditus gravely ill. God spared him, but it was clear Epaphroditus was willing to surrender everything in order to serve.

He "risked his life" that he might "complete what was deficient in your service to me," wrote Paul (2:30). There should have been others sent from Philippi. There could have been. But only Epaphroditus chose to take up the slack.

Gerald Hawthorne suggests that the Philippian church probably not only commissioned Epaphroditus to bear a financial gift to God, but had also sent him as a short-term missionary to work with Paul.[6] Staying on became impossible because of his illness. How he must have despaired when health forced him out of the lineup.

Paul urged the Philippians to greet Epaphroditus's early return with a ticker-tape parade and honor. Why? "Because on account of the work of Christ he was near even to death, having risked his life" (2:30). Second-century manuscripts suggest that the verb translated "having risked" may mean "to daringly expose oneself to danger."[7] Epaphroditus gave until he was totally spent. He chose servanthood. What a trail of trophies he must have left behind in Rome—trophies of God's grace because he cared enough to say, "Here I am! Send me!" That is living to the max.

STAY ACTIVE TILL YOU STOP

One of the surest ways to choose servanthood over selfishness in retirement is to get involved with others. You can display the mind of Christ in action. Plan ahead to be involved in meaningful activity—not just busyness.

Charles Sell and others contend that one of the most significant things a church can do is to actively involve seniors in ministry: "A sense of well-being comes from making a contribution." A sense of vocation is as essential in later years as in working days.[8]

Forced into involuntary retirement after the 1980 elections, Jimmy and Roslyn Carter discovered there is life after the White House. The Carters urge seniors to consider volunteerism: "There is something that every single one of us can do, even the busiest of younger people, but we in the 'second half' of our lives often have more time for getting involved."[9]

"But what can I do?" you ask. This question should be considered years before you retire. Barbara Deane writes that "Pre-retirees desperately need transition time to ease the terrible adjustment of going suddenly from overwork to none at all. Yet a surprisingly small percentage of people put forth the time and effort necessary to come up with a good plan."[10] Often we spend more energy and effort deciding upon vacation itineraries than we do setting goals for the rest of our lives.

The best plan for adjusting to the transition is to gradually relinquish responsibility at work, suggest Deane and others. This is how people used to live—the older they got, the more they gradually let go, eventually turning the family farm or business over to the next generation. There was no abrupt, wholesale stoppage of labor, just a gradual easing up.[11]

No matter how old you are, right now is the time to start thinking of the rest of your life. If you must quit working, what will you do? What new career does God have in mind for your senior years? A properly planned retirement can free you to serve the Lord in unique and unselfish ways that you'll find worthwhile and challenging!

A couple from Houston is learning Spanish as they prepare to retire. They plan to spend their first retirement year like Epaphroditus, assisting missionaries in the field. They've also arranged their finances so they can donate their time.

Miss Lucy Webb could have told you how to be significantly involved in the lives of others at any age. As she neared the century mark, Miss Lucy prayed faithfully and knowledgeably for the needs of others. Before her health began to fail in her nineties, she was always the first to send meals and crochet blankets and booties for young moms, volunteer for mission projects, sign up to teach.

Spunky, affectionate, spirited, Miss Lucy was never lonely and always greatly loved. She lived with her daughter and son-in-law during her final years. No mother-in-law jokes were allowed in that house. Charlie treated her like a queen. It was easy to do.

BUT WHAT CAN I DO?

Desiring to do God's will is the central issue for many of us. The Lord is famous for touching the toys that we value more than Him. He causes us to cast possessions and passions aside in favor of following Him.

For others, the problem is knowing what God wants us to do and how He wants us to do it. If we are willing, He will show us unique opportunities He has in mind for our senior years. When we say yes, He shows us what. "Delight yourself in the Lord and he will give you the desires of your heart. Commit your way to the Lord; trust in him and he will do this" (Psalm 37:4-5 NIV).

Realize this: God's work in you and through you is not finished until you are in His presence for eternity. Paul wrote that living means "fruitful labor." Thomas Chalmers, nineteenth century Scottish cleric, gave the following formula for happiness: "Something to do, something to love, and something to hope for."[12]

Martin Janis summarizes our responsibility as older adults with these words:

1. Care about others.
2. Be involved so that our brain power doesn't decline from lack of use.
3. Keep ourselves healthy so that we won't become a burden.
4. Be active in some kind of fulfilling role.[13]

To that list we might add, "See others as more important than yourself. Be anxious to serve God and others till you cross the finish line."

Abraham was no spring chicken when God called him out of Ur. It was even later in the sunset of Abraham's life when he ascended the mount, willing to sacrifice his much-loved son. The deathbed farewells of Jacob and Joseph are recorded in Scripture as evidence of significant productivity, involvement, and influence right up to the end. No matter how old you are, the Lord has a lot for you to do!

STAY IN SHAPE

Serving God is physically demanding. Conditioning will help you serve. Paul physically stressed his body to make it useful (2 Corinthians 9:27). Imagine him running the track or riding a Schwinn Airdyne and you get the picture. God gets more mileage out of us if we take care of ourselves.

Sure, we slow down as we get older. Pearl and I are finding we can't stay up as late as we used to. Nothing significant ever happens at our house after nine o'clock anymore. But we are striving to eat right, exercise, and take care of ourselves for the long haul.

Staying in shape mentally is important, too. Read. Do more than watch TV. Study. Listen to tapes. Think! And spiritually, soak up the Word of God.

Get involved with others. Too many folks are content to sit on the sidelines in the second half of life, just when their wisdom and experience are desperately needed as lights of sense in a senseless world.

IDEAS FOR INVOLVEMENT

Okay. You're in shape. Ready for the battle? Here are some ideas.

1. Discover the unique ways the Spirit of God has gifted you to operate in the body of Christ. Lists of spiritual gifts are found in Romans 12; 1 Corinthians 12; Ephesians 4; and 1 Peter 4. These gifts: encouragement, service, teaching, etc., are "body builders" of the highest order when used properly within the church. No matter your spiritual gift, you can always have a ministry of prayer, too.

2. Too many churches depend upon the preacher and paid staff to do the work of ministry. Find out how you can be involved. There is always more than enough to do. Les, a seventy-year-old former agnostic, coordinates a children's program. June is in charge of greeting and following up on visitors. Robert, a former high school coach, runs the church basketball program. The kids are fortunate to have a coach who really knows the game, and the dads learn to coach the right way. Maintenance, leadership, visitation, service projects, music ministries, food preparation, discipleship—you name it, seniors can do it!

I recommend Christian education directors be sure to include seniors in the pool of Sunday school teachers. Many churches have their own versions of Ruth and Naomi programs, where a younger and older woman are paired off as special friends, prayer partners, and encouragers for specific periods of time. Rich relationships develop as a result. You might make it a Paul and Timothy program for older and younger men, too.

3. If your church cannot use you, hundreds of parachurch organizations will put you to work. Bible Study Fellowship makes extensive use of volunteer labor. So does Stonecroft Ministries, a branch of Christian Women's Clubs International. Stonecroft conference center is staffed by retirees during the busy vacation months. Folks get to enjoy the benefit of volunteer Christian labor: cheaper rates, courteous service, Christ-minded attitudes.

You'd be surprised at the Christian organizations that would love to utilize the skills of your working days. Verne does the books for his city's local branch of Child Evangelism Fellowship, a worldwide children's ministry. Many other ministries make use of volunteer office staff, accountants, and medical personnel.

Christian camps often ask retired nurses and doctors to staff their clinics seasonally. Medical missions utilize not only physicians and nurses, but everyday folks who aren't afraid to work hard and experience new cultures. Many Christian organizations use retired salespeople as their area representatives, asking them to personally contact donors to say thanks.

Crisis pregnancy centers are desperate for volunteer counselors, particularly women; so are battered women's shelters. If you don't feel led to counsel, there are hundreds of other ways you might assist: child care, baking, sewing, shopping. (Yes, even shopping.)

You needn't look far. Decide how you might best serve God, and go for it!

4. Secular organizations make extensive use of retired volunteers, too. The AARP has a volunteer bank. SCORE (Service Corps of Retired Executives), staffed by retired businesspeople, provided over 700,000 hours of volunteer consulting to small businesses in the United States in 1990. Hospitals and nursing homes cry for volunteer labor. For what Barbara Deane calls a "smorgasbord" of volunteer ideas, check out chapter five of her *Getting Ready for a Great Retirement*. It is jammed with helpful suggestions.

5. Many seniors find it necessary to earn extra money—but not too much or their Social Security benefits may be reduced. Many retired adults find it possible to do consulting work with their former companies. Bob, retired from military service and an accounting career, loves substitute teaching in the neighborhood elementary school. He makes a positive impact on the kids and gets paid, too.

Companies like McDonald's, Wal-Mart, and Grandy's employ large numbers of seniors as hosts and hostesses. The duties are lighter than those of regular workers. True, you'll probably be overqualified for the position, but you will come in contact with people. What an opportunity to step outside your comfort zone! The workplace is an ideal environment for helping people and sharing the gospel.

My friend Tom is on his third career. After first retiring from the military and later the FAA, the former air traffic controller went back to school at age fifty-three. Now in his seventies, Tom still maintains a heating and air-conditioning repair business in his retirement community. His fees are nominal; he sees his work as a ministry. "The Lord led me into this business," Tom says.

The organization InterCristo publishes information on jobs available for people interested in working in full-time Christian service. The information is available for a price and most of the jobs described are paid positions. You might get some ideas there, too.

6. Beef up your Bible study skills so you'll be better able to evangelize, edify, and equip others. Work on memorizing specific verses as tools.

7. Invite unbelievers to a Bible study to be hosted in your home. Two great books to get you going are *Small Group Evangelism* by Richard Peace and *Life Style Evangelism* by Joseph Aldrich.

8. Use your freedom to have a ministry of hospitality. If you have a spare bedroom, volunteer to host the speakers and missionaries who visit your church. You'll come into contact with different cultures without leaving your living room.

9. Pay attention to your children and grandchildren. See how you can help. You can make an eternal difference, and caring for your own family is as much the work of Christ as pounding a pulpit. Even if you don't live as near your relatives as you'd like, there are young families in your church and neighborhood who need and want your influence.

10. Look into the possibilities of developing areas for senior ministry in your church. Think beyond creating another senior social activity group. There are plenty of those.

Elders and pastors will probably appreciate your input and willingness to help with the start-up of a new service-oriented group of seniors. Dr. Win Arn has launched a senior adult ministry called L.I.F.E. (Living in Full Effectiveness). Investigate the possibilities of incorporating his ideas into your church.

11. Don't forget to have fun! Leland F. Ryken says work and leisure are "complementary parts of the single whole of our existence."[14] You need both.

SELFISHNESS OR SERVANTHOOD?

These eleven suggestions are but a drop in the bucket of what is possible. The choice is yours. Will you, in humility, opt for the mind of Christ and the lifestyle of a servant or will you choose selfishness in your senior years?

Instead of "I've served my time. I did all that years ago. I'm too old," wouldn't it be great to hear these words from a bunch of retirees:

Sure, give me a crack at it!
I'd be happy to help.
My job is my ministry.
Do you think I could be a missionary?
Give me a towel. I want to wash some feet.

Thank God for the Pauls, Timothys, and Epaphrodituses among us who are willing to be spent on serving the real needs of real people. We need Christian seniors among us who choose the mind of Christ, the mind of service, and would have it no other way.

THANK YOU FOR GIVING TO THE LORD

Pearl and I had often heard that a Thanksgiving feast at the table of Gladys Howard was one of life's unforgettable experiences. Gladys owns the Pirate's Point resort on Little Cayman, and she graciously added us to her guest list this year. When we arrived, an elegant lady asked Pearl, "Don't I know you?"

"Yes, you are Mrs. Ball!" exclaimed Pearl.

Twenty-five years ago, Mrs. Ball had been stranded at our hometown airport. We invited her to our house, put her up for the night, and returned her to the airport after breakfast the next morning. It was a small act of kindness, but she had never forgotten our generosity, and soon the crowded room of strangers knew all about it, too.

It was a pretty good feeling. I wonder how many of us will experience similar accolades in eternity. Won't it be great to hear folks in glory express joy over the sacrificial acts of service we've done in the name of Christ? It makes everything else pale in comparison, doesn't it? Wouldn't it be great to hear a whole choir singing to you this popular refrain: "Thank you for giving to the Lord. I am a life that was changed"!

REFLECTIONS

1. Harold Clinebell describes a tombstone with this inscription: "Died at forty, buried at seventy."[15] Determine now that this won't be your epitaph.

2. Get in the habit of setting specific life goals in five-year increments.

3. If you haven't retired, choose one activity that you find

fulfilling and that doesn't involve your career. Discover ways to pursue this activity or use your work skills in retirement.

4. To make it happen you must plan it! Investigate how you'd like to spend your retirement years. Start now!

5. Review how the Lord has blessed and used you in the past. This can be a great guide for the future.

6. Maintain the spiritual disciplines of prayer and feeding upon His Word and watch God light your fire of passion to serve Him.

CHAPTER 9

DEEPENING THE RELATIONSHIP
DEVELOPING INTIMACY WITH CHRIST TO GO THE DISTANCE

How precious to me are your thoughts, O God!
How vast is the sum of them!

PSALM 139:17 NIV

People tell me youth is wasted on the young, and once I agreed. Now I say, let 'em have it. Young isn't all it's cracked up to be. I like growing up.

From my vantage, there is value in the passing of time. It takes years to develop communication and work out kinks in a marriage. It takes time for an acquaintance to develop into a friend, and years for friends to become genuinely close.

Dr. Dick Knarr is that kind of a friend. He is my all-time favorite traveling buddy—the kind of guy you could call from jail and know he won't say, "What did they get you for?" but instead will ask, "What do you want me to do?" I haven't had to test Dick's level of commitment on that one, but I've tested it in other ways.

Friendships often die when one of three things happens: 1. You are fired. 2. You fail. 3. Your family hurts.

Dick, unmoved and devoted, has stuck by me through all of these. Dick and I have camped, cared, confronted, and cried with each other for twenty-five years.

Our offices are next door to Dick's. Sometimes around half past five in the morning his voice booms from the hall leading to my office: "Coach, how about a cup of mud?" For you non-campers, that is translated, "Don, how about a cup of coffee? We need to talk." In these special times with Dick before he makes hospital rounds, I get the benefit of his wisdom and guidance. He holds me accountable, and for that I am deeply grateful.

Our friendship didn't grow overnight. We have walked through the loss of his youngest daughter, Amy, only three years old when God called her home. After all these years, Dick still can't talk about it without tears. We have been together through a host of less tragic, yet still trying situations. He probably knows me better than anyone except Pearl. I wouldn't trade the richness of our time-tested relationship for even a crack at being twenty-one again.

Others don't feel that way. Helen Gurley Brown, editor of *Cosmopolitan* magazine, writes in *The Late Show* that "the ideal state for an older woman is younger."[1] Gurley Brown found the reality of hitting her sixties so difficult that she sought professional counseling. She describes one of several sessions with psychiatrist Janet A. Kennedy (to whom the book is dedicated):

> The psychiatrist let me sob my brains out, occasionally handing me Kleenex, and when I finally stopped whining, she said, "But you want to be young!"
>
> "Of course I want to be young," I said to this dense person. "What kind of breakthrough is that?"

"Ah, but you can't be," she said. "Older is what we get."
Dr. Kennedy was seventy-three at the time. If she'd
been forty, I think I would have hit her.[2]

CAN WE STILL CUT IT?

People struggle with aging because they believe they will lose
certain abilities as they grow older. They fear they will not be able
to perform as effectively or efficiently as in younger days. A plaque
belonging to my eighty-five-year-old mom sums it up: "By the
time you get to greener pastures, you can't climb the fence."

No matter what our age, we want to be able to do what we
have always done. Much of our opinion of ourselves may
depend on it. Performance counts in our culture. We can't
escape it. Kids strive to make the grade. College students work
for a good G.P.A. Balance sheets and profit margins measure
corporate performance and productivity.

Seniors who are convinced they are less productive than
before may feel discouraged by what they perceive to be a lack
of ability to perform.

But performance is clearly overrated in our society. The
level of performance has nothing to do with the value of a person. Just because you can't do some things doesn't mean you
can't do great things (see Luke 16:15).

Scripture reveals that it's not what you do that counts with
God, it's what you are. The God of all creation and eternity is
looking for a living, growing relationship with us, not some
kind of power-packed performance!

He wants us to know Him and His Son. In the context of
that relationship, He wants to be our very best friend. What a
goal with which to finish our years!

GOD WANTS A RELATIONSHIP

A single principle defines human history: God wants a relationship with us. *Us* means you, me, and every other man, woman, and child on the planet.

Adam and Eve, the first man and woman, were created in the image of God for the purpose of having a relationship with Him. Sin altered that relationship, but the God of second chances didn't write off Adam and Eve. Even Cain, their son and the first murderer, was invited to fellowship with God (Genesis 4:6-7). This same God loved talking to Enoch so much that He snatched him straight home, bypassing the gateway of physical death (Genesis 5:24).

Noah "walked with God," and the Lord revealed the weather forecast and faxed him the blueprints of an ocean liner. The Father rescued a remnant from the destruction of the flood, when He could easily and justifiably have chucked the whole human race and started over.

God continued His plan of redemption with a simple shepherd named Abraham, promising him a nation, a land, and an eternal descendant who would bless "all peoples on earth" (Genesis 12:3). The same God who gave baby Isaac to Abraham and Sarah later answered Isaac's prayers with twin boys: Jacob and Esau. The same God followed Joseph from pit to prison to the palace in Egypt, assuring the rescue of the young Hebrew nation from famine.

This God commissioned Gideon, inspired Samuel, revealed Himself to Nathan, anointed David. He gave victory to the undertakings of Joshua, Ezra, and Nehemiah. He walked with Daniel in the lions' den. He empowered a host of prophets like Isaiah, Micah, Jeremiah, and Ezekiel.

Thousands of years after He was rejected by Adam and Eve in the garden, God reached down into human history to link up with us again by sending His Son to walk among us. Jesus is God in human form. We could touch, feel, and see Him. His earthly ministry was rich in relationships: Mary, Martha, Lazarus, Mary Magdalene, the Disciples, Nicodemus, Zacchaeus. Anyone who was lost could be found by Him. Tax collectors, children, lepers, prostitutes, the broken, bleeding, and frail—no one was excluded.

Neither is anyone who honestly seeks Him excluded today (2 Peter 3:9).

THE PERFORMANCE TRAP: THE FREEWAY TO HELL

Many people believe they can be good enough apart from Christ to be acceptable to God. Many nice guys die with that thought and experience eternity away from the presence of God.

Hell is no mythical place. Nor is it a neighborhood bar, a place filled with clones of your mother-in-law, or the same thing as heaven. One person's heaven is not another's hell. Hell is hell, a place of total separation, and you won't like it if you go there.

A recent "Far Side" cartoon depicts two guys standing at hell's gate, coffee mugs in their hands. "They thought of everything," one says. "Even the coffee is cold." Anyone who is relying on good performance to get to heaven has much more to worry about than cold coffee. Unless we humble ourselves before God and accept the provision He has made for us in His Son, reservations for our eternal destination are made...and they aren't for heaven.

DO YOU REALLY KNOW CHRIST?

In senior adulthood, most of us will have the time to pursue a vital relationship with the Lord Jesus Christ as never before. We can really get to know Him!

Really knowing Christ does not involve memorizing facts, figures, and historical infobytes. The facts of His life are of no importance to us if we aren't ready to make a commitment to Him. "That's nice for those who need it," replied one senior after I shared the gospel one day. He still didn't get it!

Truly knowing Christ first involves coming to Him by faith. You must believe that through His perfect life and His undeserved death on the cross and separation from God, He paid the penalty you deserve for your sins (Romans 5:8). Once you trust Christ as Savior, you are in a relationship with Him for eternity.

But you still can ignore Him.

Part two of really knowing Christ is establishing fellowship, authentic friendship, with Him. He is ever waiting, arms open to embrace you. A growing relationship with the Lord demands discipline, desire, dedication, direction, openness, and availability. It takes a significant amount of what many senior adults have in spades: time. It is one of the most worthwhile investments of hours and energy imaginable.

RELIGION SAYS DO! SALVATION SAYS DONE!

In a deepening relationship with Him, we discover what brings our Father delight. Religion says "Do!" Salvation says "Done!" Relationship says, "Delight!"

The apostle Paul understood that the temptation to perform to please God was great. He cautioned his Philippian friends to "Beware of the dogs, beware of the evil workers; beware of the false circumcision" (3:2).

"Dogs" referred to the Judaizers—those who taught that certain rites and ceremonies had to be performed in accordance with Jewish law if salvation were to be secured. This legalism was a profound problem. Evidently Paul had received fresh word of the spread of such thought among the Philippians. He was concerned. His language is strong. The word "dogs" doesn't refer to cute harmless puppies but to ravenous creatures roaming the streets in packs. It was the same word Jews used when referring to Gentiles.

J. B. Lightfoot writes, "These Judaizers were dogs because they greedily devoured the garbage of carnal ordinances or laws, the very refuse of God's table."[3] Table scraps—that's all the requirements of God's law are when you know God's Son. The law is like a mirror. It shows us our need. The law has been called a schoolmaster to lead us to Christ. The law only condemns, convicts, and crucifies. Salvation is a gracious gift. When you trust Christ, you receive what God has freely provided to meet your need.

Paul also warned against "evil workers"—false teachers clouding the presentation of the gospel. Today cults, non-Christian religions, self-help gurus, the occult sciences—all give people the message that they can somehow become good enough for God through human performance, if God matters at all.

Finally, Paul warned against "false circumcision." The term refers to physical circumcision. The Judaizers were convinced there was spiritual value in physical circumcision and that this mark of God's promises to Abraham was essential before one could experience the blessings of God. They called for all who would be Christians to undergo this ceremonial rite. Ouch! They called for cutting the flesh to demonstrate devotion to God. Again, the lie proclaimed was that human performance could make people right with God.

'Taint so. Never has been.

The prophet Elijah could tell us all about that. He watched as the priests of Baal tried to convince their god to send fire from heaven to burn up a sacrifice. All day long the priests begged Baal to smoke it. They wailed, cried, and slashed their wrists till the blood flowed freely. It was all for nothing. Their god did not exist and the one true God was not impressed. Only when Elijah, humbly and in faith, asked the Lord to ignite a waterlogged bull did God unleash His power. Elijah didn't have to gash himself, dance, or wail to please God. He simply had to ask Him to act (1 Kings 18:36-38).

CUTTING THE HEART

For those of us who desire to know Jesus Christ deeply and intimately, the issue is not a cutting of the flesh, but a cutting of the heart (Romans 2:29). Moses spoke of the circumcision of the heart in his farewell address (Deuteronomy 30:6). Elsewhere in Scripture we read, "For in Christ Jesus neither circumcision nor uncircumcision means anything, but faith working through love (Galatians 5:6). Later in Galatians we read of the hypocrisy of those who would require believers to be physically circumcised and of the meaninglessness of that action (Galatians 6:13-15). The circumcision of the Christian is not a physical act at all, but a change of heart wrought by the work of the Spirit of God in us.

Jesus said of genuine, growing believers, "You will know them by their fruits" (Matthew 7:20). In Philippians 3:3, Paul mentioned three symptoms we'll display if we have a circumcised heart, a heart to know Christ:

1. We worship in the Spirit of God.
2. We glory in Christ Jesus.
3. We place no confidence in the flesh.

Growing Christians are those who are leaving God in, not locking Him out. They do not depend upon their human abilities to perform in a way that will please Him or fulfill His will.

Ask Abraham. He sure messed things up with Hagar trying to make a nation on his own. You'd think he might have at least checked on Medicare maternity benefits. God had plans to work through a geriatric wife, not a sweet young Egyptian thing. Sarah and Abraham received a bundle from the stork in God's time, not theirs. The promises depended upon God (Romans 4:1-3,20-21).

King Hezekiah got it right. Speaking to a crowd scared silly by Sennacherib and the forces of Assyria who had come down to conquer Judah, these were his words: "Do not be afraid or discouraged...for there is a greater power with us than with him. With him is only the arm of flesh, but with us is the Lord our God to help us and to fight our battles" (2 Chronicles 32:7-8 NIV).

My buddy Les had it right, too. Formerly our community's most outspoken agnostic, Les only accompanied his wife to church to please her. Incredibly, Les announced after services one Sunday, "Don, I want to be baptized!"

"Whoa, Les," I answered. "Let's not put the cart before the horse. Why?"

"In church today, the lens finally came into focus. I realized Jesus died for me. I can do nothing to achieve heaven except trust that which He has already done!"

Les had recognized and personalized the single truth upon which each person's destiny hinges. He had believed Christ and realized he could place no confidence in human performance to become righteous before God.

ONE DOOR AND ONLY ONE

Like Les, adults of all ages have a tough time comprehending that God is not interested in ability and action but in acceptance of His gift and availability for Him to do His work through them. Many use the freedom of retirement to plunge into worthwhile projects they believe will make them acceptable to God. Delivering meals on wheels, fund-raising, volunteering are all good things, but none are what God really wants if He doesn't have your heart. He wants you (Revelation 3:20).

Ray is such a man. Active in fraternal organizations and service clubs, his battle cry is, "We take a good man and make him better." Ray has a keen intellect, is a community leader and a superb golfer. Scanning his accomplishments, we'd think, "What a man!"

But Ray has a big problem. There is a skunk in the woodpile. He is confused about relationship and performance and hasn't grasped the fact that salvation is a gift through faith. Constantly he wonders if he is doing enough to make God sit up and take notice. His drinking is increasing in proportion to his fear of death. At the heart of it all is a deadening pride that tells Ray he can go it alone.

God won't care how much money we donated to the underprivileged, how many great and noble tasks we undertook in His name, how many food drives we engineered, how many offices we held, if we do not know Him.

More's the pity, too, when a *believer* doesn't get to know his God. It's possible to receive the Lord Jesus as Savior in an act of faith, then turn right around and attempt to perform in the flesh to please Him (Galatians 3:3). How ironic that we trust Him for our destiny but not for daily living. We still think we have to perform for Him. So we plunge ourselves into projects. We busy ourselves with activities. We may even be pretty hard workers in church. But we are not propelled by God's plan, presence, and person as much as by a sense of duty. We do some of the right things without the right motivation. We operate in the flesh even though we are saved.

Just as with the priests of Baal at Elijah's Mount Carmel convention, God is not impressed.

NOTES FROM A RELIGIOUS SUPER ACHIEVER

We know God is not impressed with human performance, because if anyone could impress Him like this, it would have been Paul. The apostle described himself in Philippians 3:4-6 as a member of the tribe of Benjamin, a full-blooded Hebrew born to Hebrew parents who had obeyed the Jewish law by having Paul circumcised at eight days of age. From the very start, Paul was a good Jewish boy.

Paul was also a Pharisee, an elite group of six thousand within the Jewish nation sworn to zealously uphold the Mosaic law. Paul needed no pushing to perform the minutiae of the law; he lived and breathed it.

Seeing the upstart religion of Christianity as a threat to his beloved Judaism, Paul actively participated in its persecution. Stephen's murderers laid their cloaks at his feet. He headed for Damascus with intentions of crushing the young church.

Paul was passionate about the traditions of his Jewish faith: "As to the righteousness which is in the Law, found blameless" (Philippians 3:6). In Galatians 1:14, he described himself this way: "I was advancing in Judaism beyond many of my contemporaries among my countrymen, being more extremely zealous for my ancestral traditions." He outstripped the pack in terms of human holiness. If anyone could become righteous before God by performance, it was Paul.

Then he learned that relationship was what counted: "But whatever things were gain to me, those things I have counted as loss for the sake of Christ" (Philippians 3:7). All the good deeds, all the religious observances, all the bleeding to climb the mountain to God, weren't good enough.

Religion is a favorite hobby of the flesh. The "I will" of the flesh loves to achieve for its own satisfaction and glory. Paul learned what all of us must. When it comes to keeping His law, God doesn't grade on a curve.

What matters to God? Relationship. Paul wrote, "I count all things to be loss in view of the surpassing value of knowing Christ Jesus my Lord, for whom I have suffered the loss of all things, and count them but rubbish in order that I may gain Christ" (Philippians 3:8).

Knowing Christ—that's what matters. All else is garbage, worthless. Like the prodigal son, Paul "came to his senses."

We all lose our lives for something. Paul chose to lose his for Jesus Christ. He would be broken, spilled out, shattered for the Savior, if necessary. But these acts of loving sacrifice would not make him holy or holier. Only Jesus Christ could do that.

THE KNOWLEDGE OF CHRIST

It was the knowledge of Jesus which Paul found to be of "surpassing value" (Philippians 3:8). The word translated "knowing" in this verse signifies more than a superficial acquaintance. It suggests personal, intimate knowledge. So does the verb *ginosko* which Paul used in verse 10: "That I may know Him [by personal experience], and the power of His resurrection and the fellowship of His sufferings, being conformed to His death." The apostle spoke of intimate knowledge born of shared experience: deep knowledge which is the result of spending extensive time with someone or doing something. Paul wanted to know Christ, with all that knowing Christ involved.

Paul's prayer would not have been, "Lord, I want to know about You," but "Lord, I want to know You!" Let me feel what You feel. Let me share Your heart, Your passion, Your desire.

It's important to note that the apostle never felt he had arrived and that nothing more could be done or learned of Christ. Romans 11:33 reveals the glories that await those who faithfully pursue the path of deeper intimacy with God: "Oh, the depth of the riches both of the wisdom and knowledge of God! How unsearchable are His judgments and unfathomable His ways!"

On our first visit to Grand Cayman, our hosts Doug and Sara took us out on a dive boat. The marine biologist who was our guide gave me a short resort course so I could qualify for the fifty-foot dive.

What a glorious experience! Coral, fish, conch! I saw a sea turtle, barracuda, and a rare eagle ray. Before we surfaced, the dive master took me to the north wall of an underwater chasm. Thousands of feet of water gave way beneath me, making me realize how little we had seen and know!

That's the way it is with Jesus. It just gets richer and richer.

GETTING THERE

The knowledge of Christ results from time spent in the Scriptures and with the Lord in communion and prayer. "Getting to know you, getting to know all about you," could have been my friend Les's theme song after he came to Christ in faith. He plunged into God's Word with a rare enthusiasm. Immediately he entered a discipleship program with me involving Bible studies geared for new believers and an organized Scripture memory system. It wasn't long before Les had read through the *One Year Bible* and had committed one hundred verses to memory. We worked our way through theology texts.

Within three years he had memorized more than two hundred Bible verses, reviewing them as he worked out daily on a rowing machine. He was seventy-two years old at his conversion, and by the time he was seventy-four, he had developed an intimate relationship with the Lord Jesus.

Discipleship is costly. Paul knew it would involve suffering. It means the sacrifice of time and personal preferences. It may entail physical or financial or emotional suffering.

Yet it will be worth it all to know Christ deeply and intimately.

TRANSITIONS

What a unique opportunity senior adulthood brings for us to get to know Christ in a very personal, private way. Paul B. Maves suggested that the years from fifty-five to sixty-four be a time of anticipation and preparation for most of us.[4] It can be a time of reassessing values and determining the direction of the rest of our lives. It's a prime occasion to commit ourselves to place knowing Christ above everything else.

Tim Stafford labeled Paul's advice in Philippians 3:7-9 as a "shift of values...essential to the Christian life."[5] It is a shift that is thrust upon most older Christians, as the process of aging forces us to let go of much of our past. Rather than simply pondering what purpose our lives have served, Stafford recommends we think about what purpose life yet holds. He calls the first process, "life review," and the second, "life preview," and urges seniors to ask themselves, "If given two more years, or twenty, what do I want to do with my life?... What story should these remaining years tell my children and grandchildren? As an old tree, what new shoots do I hope to produce?"[6]

May there be among these new shoots a greater intimacy with Jesus. Knowing Him involves abiding in Him. Jesus said in John 15:5, "I am the vine, you are the branches; he who abides in Me, and I in him, he bears much fruit; for apart from Me you can do nothing." The branch cannot bear fruit unless it is connected to the vine and drawing sustenance from the vine. Abiding means:

1. Drawing upon all that Christ is.
2. Depending upon all that He can do.
3. Developing into His likeness.

LETTING GO

Before we are prepared to grow in intimacy with Jesus Christ, two things must happen.

1. We must forget the past. Paul wrote to the Philippians that he was "forgetting what lies behind" (3:13). Too many seniors are shrouded in unburied pasts. So what if you've blown it a time or two or twenty? So what if you've tripped up on the track? You can still get up and finish. So what if you tossed away the ball on a critical play? You still have the rest of the game to play.

If anyone had reason for regret, it was Paul. Satan could easily have manipulated his guilt over Stephen's death and his persecution of the church into a gigantic stop sign to spiritual growth. When Paul first became a Christian, people didn't trust him. They were scared of him. How easily his previous sins and mistakes might have reared up to mar the present. His past was embarrassing. Shameful! But Paul knew even a lifetime of denying God could be cleared from the slate. As Billy Zeoli said, "Our God has a big eraser."

Solomon advised letting go of the past: "Do not say, 'Why were the old days better than these?' For it is not wise to ask such questions" (Ecclesiastes 7:10). Trust me, the good old days...weren't. Forget the tarnished past.

Don't dwell too much on the good stuff, either. There is a temptation for seniors to rest on past laurels rather than seek new crowns. Don't attempt to erase your memories—just learn from them and go on. Don't get wiped out by them or stuck in them.

From a practical standpoint, dwelling on the past makes us reminisce, and other people's capacity to absorb our nostalgia is far less than our capacity to tell them about it. People want to hear what God has done for you lately!

Another aspect of letting go of the past is forgiveness. Paul forgave John Mark. Peter forgave Paul. Stephen forgave his killers. Jesus forgave us all on the cross.

Dwight D. Eisenhower made a practice of recording on paper the names of men who injured or wronged him, then crumpling the slip and dropping it into a lower desk drawer. Recalled the President, "It seemed to be effective and helped me avoid harboring useless black feelings."[7]

My friend Les could easily have become stuck regretting the past. I mentioned he was our community's leading agnostic. Talk about ornery! Once a minister visited Les in the hospital to pray before major surgery. Les would only let him pray if he agreed to leave off the words, "In Jesus' name." After his conversion, Les wisely refused to let what he had been affect where he was going with Jesus.

2. We must also press on. Paul said he was "reaching forward to what lies ahead" (3:13). Rosalie Harper, for thirty-eight years a director of attendance for her city's schools, learned to do just that. She writes, "I choose to go on living a rich, full life.... If I ever find myself looking backward instead of forward, I will just say out loud: 'Pardon me, is my retirement showing?'"[8]

The question is not what has been, but what will be. From now till check-out time are the years which count. Les has three desires. He is fervently praying he will lead someone to Christ. He wants to disciple that person in the faith for at least a year. He longs to keep on discovering all there is to discover about his friend, Jesus.

IT WILL BE WORTH IT ALL

Paul summed up this section of his letter by saying, "I press on toward the goal for the prize of the upward call of God in Christ Jesus" (3:14). The verb "press on" means "to run straight toward."[9] No distractions. No alternate objectives.

A poster on my office wall contains this statement by Dame Margot Fonteyn: "The runner who puts the last ounce of effort into the race feels the glorious satisfaction of having given everything to the moment." Paul, the original New Testament goal setter, was running for the finish line, the "upward call of God." That race does not stop at retirement or in senior adulthood, but only intensifies the closer we get to the tape.

Nearly all of the senior adult literature I read recommends establishing tangible goals as a means of negotiating a successful retirement. Paul Fremont Brown writes that people without attitude problems in retirement are ones whose lives are characterized by absorbing interests or goals that give a lasting feeling of fulfillment. Such men and women live for something outside of themselves that they feel is important.[10]

For the Christian, maximum fulfillment will only come as we use the rest of our lives to cooperate fully with God's ultimate purpose of making us more like His Son. Part of that necessitates getting to know that Son.

Like Les, why not set goals in the area of knowing Jesus? Here are a few suggestions:

1. Develop short-term goals related to the overall goal of knowing Christ. Set out to study a section of Scripture or memorize a series of verses. You won't be performing to try to please God, just taking tangible steps to get better acquainted with His Son. Little goals, met, add up to big achievements.

2. Ask God to give you an attitude of gratitude about all the changes which are occurring.

3. Search the present to see if it is being negatively affected by the past. Is there someone you need to forgive? Some episodes you need to set aside? Some accomplishments you are so proud of that you are comfortable resting upon what has been already done? Ask God to help you put these behind you and press on.

4. Check your motives. Are you performing in some way to attempt to please God? Be sure you have understood and acted upon the single condition of salvation: trusting Jesus Christ.

5. Recognize that even in suffering, God is helping you conform to the image of His Son. Your knowledge of Christ is increasing in every trial.

REFLECTIONS

1. No matter what your age, practice the spiritual disciplines of prayer, Bible study, and Scripture memory.

2. Never be satisfied with your level of Christian growth or commitment.

3. Is there someone you need to forgive or something you need to forget? Refuse to let the past negatively affect the present.

4. Get involved in serious Bible study and Scripture memory now!

5. If appropriate, encourage your parents to become involved in serious Bible study and Scripture memory.

6. Scrutinize your motives in undertaking new activities. Are you trying somehow to perform to please God?

CHAPTER 10

EVIDENCE THAT THE KING IS IN RESIDENCE

KEEPING THE JOY

𝓋

Some cause happiness wherever they go. Some, whenever they go.

SPOTLIGHT

The news report shocked the nation, so strange were the circumstances of her death. CNN and the major networks covered her demise as no one had covered her life. Adele Gaboury's body was found in her Worcester, Massachusetts, residence the second time police officers entered the home to look for her. She had evidently lain dead on her kitchen floor for four years, her lifeless frame obscured by clutter and garbage. No one had missed her.

Years before, neighbors had noticed something strange about the Gaboury house. The lawn was unkempt; mail and newspapers accumulated. They contacted Ms. Gaboury's brother, who after a cursory check of area nursing homes, concluded Adele was a patient in one. He never visited the home to discover his mistake. Since their mother's death in 1979, the family had not been close, explained the brother.

187

Neighbors mowed Adele's lawn. A utility worker entered her basement to shut off the water when pipes burst. Another neighbor advised the post office to discontinue delivery when hundreds of unopened letters spilled out Adele's front door. No one suspected Adele's body was inside, positioned near a telephone as if the seventy-three-year-old had been attempting to make a call when she died of natural causes in 1989.

"She didn't want anyone bothering her at all. She just wanted to be left alone. I guess she got her wish, but it's awfully sad," said June Tsiokas, an old friend of Gaboury.

"She was rather a private person," said Gaboury's former employer. "She kept her own affairs to herself."

"My heart bleeds for her, but you can't blame a soul," said neighbor Rose Girouard. "If she saw you out there, she never said hello to you."[1]

Was Adele Gaboury shy? Eccentric? Bitter? Was she like Dennis the Menace's Mr. Wilson, a grumpy but harmless misanthrope? Did she long for someone who cared? What made her tick? We'll never know.

We can guess that her life brimmed with silent pain. She seemed to have showered little goodwill on others, and she experienced little of it herself. For four years the world easily overlooked the fact that she was no longer in it.

Not so with my buddy Dub, a lovable, retired school administrator. Oh, how he loved to tease about sleeping through my sermons! Dub's life was not without grief: He buried two children and a wife. "My cup is overflowing!" remained his constant, joyous exclamation. And it did. He died recently, and his widow's reflection said it all, "Dub is where he wanted to be."

Clemmo keeps up the joy, too. Folks love to be around him. He likes to tell of visiting his old high school and walking to the second floor to examine the rows of framed pictures of graduating classes from years past. He turned from studying the photo of his class to find a young boy studying him. "Can you find me in that picture, son?" asked Clemmo. The boy looked and looked till finally Clemmo pointed himself out.

"Boy, time sure made a mess of you, mister!" exclaimed the kid. Clemmo just roared with laughter.

WHERE HAS ALL THE JOY GONE?

Happiness. Joy. It's what everyone wants and so few seem to consistently have. Parents constantly pipe the message to kids beginning careers and choosing mates: "More than anything, we want you to be happy."

When people decide to divorce, they often say, "I'm just not happy anymore in this relationship. There's got to be more."

We all know the stereotypical image of the grumpy, groaning senior. The crotchety old guy no one likes, the dried up prune of a woman who looks as if she'd swallowed an egg and is waiting for it to hatch. Occasionally a human tragedy like that of Adele Gaboury surfaces to convince us that the stereotypes are right and that growing old has got to be arduous, joyless, lonely, and pathetic.

Not true. There is potentially even more joy in the last stretch of track than when we first started. There's always joy when you get a promotion! Joy when you marry! Joy when you see friends and family! Joy is an attainable goal as we get close to home, too.

WANTED: CHRISTIAN HEDONISTS

What we need in order to attack the second half of life is a little Christian hedonism. Make that a lot. The final holes on life's golf course can be the most fun. With a plan you can par, birdie, or maybe even eagle the last one—or better yet, ace it. Believe it.

Hedonism is a dirty word in Christian culture. It evokes images of decadence, indulgence, and sensuality. We have spoken negatively of the dangers of too much hedonism in this very book. Leisure-laden retirement lifestyles do not bring lasting satisfaction. But a happy balance can be struck.

Sometimes we Christians react to the world's abuses of the quest for joy and happiness by refusing to feel any ourselves. We are almost afraid to have fun, to let down, live it up, and laugh. To do so might seem "unspiritual." This mind-set is in direct contrast to Paul's repeated exhortations: "Rejoice in the Lord always; again I will say rejoice" (Philippians 4:4).

Christians are supposed to have fun.

Christ wants us to experience His joy.

We need what John Piper calls Christian hedonism, a philosophy of life built upon five convictions he lists in *Desiring God*:

1. The longing to be happy is a universal human experience, and it is good, not sinful.
2. We should never try to deny or resist our longing to be happy, as though it were a bad impulse. Instead we should seek to intensify this longing and nourish it with whatever will provide the deepest and most enduring satisfaction.

3. The deepest and most enduring happiness is found only in God.
4. The happiness we find in God reaches its consummation when it is shared with others in the manifold ways of love.
5. To the extent we try to abandon the pursuit of our own pleasure, we fail to honor God and love people. Or, to put it positively: the pursuit of pleasure is a necessary part of all worship and virtue. That is, the chief end of man is to glorify God *by* enjoying him forever.[2]

Piper also quotes from a sermon preached by C. S. Lewis in 1941, calling it one of the most important readings he encountered in his journey toward Christian hedonism:

If there lurks in most modern minds the notion that to desire our own good and earnestly to hope for the enjoyment of it is a bad thing, I submit that this notion has crept in from Kant and the Stoics and is no part of the Christian faith. Indeed, if we consider the unblushing promises of reward and the staggering nature of the rewards promised in the Gospels, it would seem that our Lord finds our desires, not too strong, but too weak. We are half-hearted creatures, fooling around with drink and sex and ambition when infinite joy is offered us, like an ignorant child who wants to go on making mud pies in a slum because he cannot imagine what is meant by the offer of a holiday at the sea. We are far too easily pleased.[3]

Piper concludes from Lewis that, "The enemy of worship is not that our desire for pleasure is too strong but too weak!" We settle for second best. A home and family, a job, a few friends, a TV, a microwave, an occasional night out, an annual vacation, maybe a new personal computer—these satisfy us. According to Piper, "We have accustomed ourselves to such meager, short-lived pleasures that our capacity for joy has shriveled."[4]

EPISTLES OF JOY

Real, God-given joy springs to life in the self-denying, serving heart. Selfish pursuits only stifle and shrivel joy. Selfishness leaves senior adults hollow. Toys aren't enough. God gives us a tremendous capacity for deep, abiding pleasure in Him and His Word. He also gives us the ability to enjoy the earth, ourselves, and other people. It is we who satisfy ourselves with the shallow and the superficial: golf scores and board games rather than meaningful relationships. Junk instead of joy.

God longs for us to be joyful. Truly happy. Truly content. Truly grateful. Enjoying ourselves with a mix of pleasure and purpose. The life of a believer is designed to be an epistle of joy even in the face of adversity.

Have you ever been awakened by a long tongue licking your ear, slobbers and whiskers brushing your face? Feeling four points of pressure on your shoulder lets you know the puppy wants to share her joy of living with you! Oh boy. Eagerly she bounces from person to person, exhilarated by each new target. If only we could give away that same joy with reckless abandon!

We draw sustaining joy from knowing God is in control. The channels of joy open as we focus on God's Word, staying close through prayer and depending upon His Spirit to produce joy in us.

Like love, joy is not merely an emotion. It is the result of a relationship. Joy knows God and that He always triumphs. Joy knows this isn't all there is to life. Joy knows a place is being prepared. Joy knows that all we are going through is only getting us ready for that place. Joy knows that each day only brings us closer to that fabulous destiny. Joy intensifies when we see others join the family of God through faith. Joy understands each day that this is the day the Lord has made.

JOY IS

Joy in the life of a believer in Christ is evidence of at least four qualities:

1. Joy is a sign of salvation. Psalm 16:11 states, "You have made known to me the path of life; you will fill me with joy in your presence, with eternal pleasures at your right hand" (NIV). Genuine, abiding joy indicates we have a right relationship with the Father through Jesus the Son. How thrilling it is that our sins are forgiven and our debt paid!

When we are saved, we receive the gift of God's own Spirit. Joy is a fruit of His power and presence in us (Galatians 5). This is stuff to get excited about! Luke writes that the early Christians were "continually filled with joy and with the Holy Spirit" (Acts 13:52).

"I found Him late, but I found Him!" joyfully exclaimed a senior I had the privilege of leading to Christ. What a rare breed: Statistics on the percentage of folks who respond to the gospel after sixty are not encouraging. But this guy beat the odds and found the joy of His salvation.

193

2. Joy is a result of fellowship with the Father. Joy is a primary evidence of a life in focused fellowship, communion, and friendship with the Father (1 John 1:3-4). As the Lord becomes our best friend, as we abide in Him, walk with Him, learn more of Him and His love for us, we discover our joy in Him. The Spirit of God produces this joy which wells up inside us (John 7:37-38). The equation goes like this:

Submission to His will
<u>+ Obedience to His Word</u>
Joy produced by His Spirit

After King David's moral failure he felt estranged from God. Psalm 32:3-4 describes how David suffered physically: "When I kept silent, my bones wasted away through my groaning all day long." His arthritis flared up and was killing him. David also suffered spiritually: "For day and night your hand was heavy upon me." God's hand was upon him in displeasure and discipline. Emotionally he was hurting. too: "My strength was sapped as in the heat of summer." David had spent vast emotional energy rationalizing his mistakes.

"Restore to me the joy of your salvation," he begs (Psalm 51:12 NIV). The distance David felt from God, his closest friend, was the self-induced product of sin. He lost the joy.

Perhaps the first thing to fall by the wayside when we are out of fellowship with God is our joy. If you don't feel like you are on speaking terms with the Father, the reason you have parted company may be one of many: ongoing sin, refusal to spend significant time with Him in His Word and prayer, failure to respond to His authority.

Whatever the reason, you have moved away from Him. He'd never desert you, one of His children. In the garden, it was Adam and Eve who withdrew and broke their appointment with God. In the parable, the prodigal's father waits, watches, and never stops wanting the restoration of the close relationship with the son who has wandered astray.

When we feel distant from God, He loves, longs, and looks for us to respond so He can restore the intimacy. The Master's voice calls, but like disobedient pups we hide in the yard or slink toward Him on our bellies, reluctant and ashamed. That's a rotten way to live when the joy of the Lord is available to us.

I have seen God restore the joy in cases where addictive behaviors, interpersonal problems, and botched-up priorities interfered. Never doubt He can do it.

3. Joy indicates a right response to trials. "Consider it all joy, my brethren, when you encounter various trials," wrote James, the brother of Jesus (James 1:2). Taking joy in the Lord is the proper response to the storms of life. Joy is a manifestation of our submission to the One who does all things well.

When I told Pearl a few years ago that I was going to write a commentary on the New Testament book of James, she exclaimed, "Lord help us all! You know whenever you preach or teach on James, we get to practice it!" We were in the car at the time and I laughed so hard I nearly drove off the road. She was right.

Our God reigns...and rains. The proper response to anything He allows is joy. Joy is knowing God is there and has promised not to go away, no matter what (Hebrews 13:5).

Joy in the face of suffering and trials is having confidence in God, an exhilaration in His power, an anticipation of His deliverance, an appreciation of His teachings. Joy is being an example to others.

Real joy doesn't demand, "Why, God, did you let this happen?" Real joy asks, "Okay, Lord, what am I supposed to learn from this? I look forward with joy and expectation to the results of this curriculum You've designed for me. How can I grow through this? How can I give glory to You?"

Real joy seeks the big picture. It sees beyond the circumstances to the benefits of changed character, increased trust, certain victory. Jesus could see beyond immediate trials and "for the joy set before Him endured the cross" (Hebrews 12:2). He felt good about the greater good that would issue from His sacrifice.

4. Joy signals a right response to heaven. Thoughts of what is beyond the finish line are cause for great joy, too. How tremendous it will be to stand before the Lord Jesus, our race done, our reward ahead. Always the apostle Paul kept a proper perspective of heaven.

Paul calls the Philippians his "joy and crown" (Philippians 4:1). He is filled with joy as he thinks of what the good news of Christ has accomplished in Philippi. His arrest there with Silas led to the spread of the gospel. What a thrill it was to watch God shift the momentum and snatch victory from the jaws of defeat as Paul and Silas's jailer became one of the first Philippian converts. Folks would be in heaven because of what God had done through Paul, and Paul delighted in that, knowing he'd receive an eternal crown.

Being down and out isn't so bad if it gets you looking up. Salvation among seniors often occurs on the beds of affliction. Tear-filled eyes and broken voices respond to God's offer, and heaven becomes a reality. Joy replaces fear as eternity comes in view and death draws nigh.

METHODS OF MAINTAINING THE JOY

But how do I stay joyful these days? What about when the bloodsuckers, as the late columnist Lewis Grizzard called them, line up at my hospital door wanting another sample? I've been there. When they can't find a vein, I feel like shouting, "I gave at the office!"

And what about when you run out of checks before you run out of month? When your dog has to be put to sleep? Your granddaughter turns up pregnant? Your car dies a natural death at 140,000 miles just when the washer and dryer both go on strike? Your wife tells you to look for work?

You can still hang on to your joy.

Stand Firm. To hang on to joy, Paul advised the Philippians: "So stand firm in the Lord" (4:1). Refuse to throw in your hand or quit early.

Here I stand! God help me! Say it! Let the world see Christ in your convictions, character, and courage. When the howling hurricanes of aging beat up on your frail frame, may it be said: He still stands! The storm has spent its fury, and there he is, the only one left standing. Persecution, problems, and pressure make us think, "It's not worth it." Standing firm says, "Yes it is."

I have heard that engraved upon a stone on the village green in Lexington, Massachusetts, are the words of Captain Parker who commanded the colonial forces in the memorable battle fought there in 1776: "Stand your ground, don't fire unless fired upon. But if they mean to have a war, let it begin here."

Satan rolls out his heavy artillery against seniors. He would like nothing better than for us to hang it up spiritually in the home stretch. He loves for us to doubt our relationship with God, forsake fellowship with Him, rail in anger at Him for our trials, and forget all about the joys just around the bend in the place He has gone to prepare.

Forgive, Forget. Remember Euodia and Syntyche, two bat-tleaxes hacking away at each other in the Philippian church? If Satan can't stop us from rejoicing over all God has promised, he can always turn our eyes to the faults of others. "Jeepers, Mr. Wilson," Dennis might say. "Why are you so angry?"

It's hard to have the joy of the Lord when you give in to the temptation to criticize others. Lack of forgiveness is a surefire joy stopper. If Christians don't hang together, they'll hang sep-arately. When you find yourself disagreeing with another, ask yourself how important the issue really is. Be willing to forgive and forget. Stand firm in the refusal to let differences with oth-ers ruin your joy. Be a peacemaker.

The crusty old gentleman walked up after Bible class one evening. Tears spilled from his eyes. He had held a grudge for more than a year over a misunderstanding at his church. He'd dropped out of things, was about to resign his membership. He refused to talk to the pastor about it. Yet there he was, crying in grief and brokenness as he realized that as Christ had forgiven him, so he must forgive the ones with whom he had been in conflict. He longed to re-open the stopped-up wells of joy. And joy flowed freely in the face of forgiveness.

"What's eating you?" we ask. Failure to forgive is a kind of cannibalism—you feed on the rotting flesh of yesterday. When the past quarrels with the present, there can be no future. Paul recommended that Clement and others in the Philippian church intervene as peacemakers to help Euodia and Syntyche resolve their differences (4:3).

Is there another person you are allowing to rob you of joy? Why should you let the actions and attitudes of anyone do that? Stamp paid-in-full on the invoices of those you believe have wronged you. Forgive and forget and get on with the joy of living!

Rejoice in the Lord. Another method of maintaining joy is to remember where it is to be placed. Stolen joy is often misfocused joy. People will disappoint us. Products will fail. Performances will be lacking. But our joy, if directed properly, will be sustained.

The direction in question is *up.* We are to rejoice in the Lord. God is the object of Christian joy.[5] He never disappoints or fails us.

Cultivate an Attitude of Gratitude. To rejoice in the Lord, be grateful. Grateful people are awake to the power of God and recognize from whose hand all things come. They count their blessings even as they are nailed to the wall because they know things could be tougher and that God has some truths to teach them.

Grateful people avoid unrealistic expectations. They see even difficulties as opportunities to live, to love, to learn, and to grow. "Looking back on my seventy-three years," remarked my friend Sid, "I'm glad for all I've experienced and I'm looking forward to what is ahead." What an attitude of gratitude!

Keep your Growing Edge. People finding their joy in the Lord also maintain a growing edge. They are attuned to God's plan and see the possibilities of spiritual growth even in the most challenging situations.

Sid, the fellow who is so happy to be alive, has faced unexpected financial reversals in retirement. He isn't letting his circumstances get him down. "You're not really retired, are you?" I joked with him the other day. "Nope. Not as long as the bills say, 'Pay me,'" he chuckled in reply as he headed out to complete a carpentry job to earn extra money.

Know God's Grace. Joyful Christians also know God's grace—not just positionally but experientially. They are not only saved by grace, they act like it! They realize that when God says, "My grace is sufficient for you, for power is perfected in weakness," He means it (2 Corinthians 12:9). In the dark of the night when our little ship is taking on water, adequate grace is there. Grace for the early retirement, the unexpected divorce, the emergency surgery.

Realize Your Joy Is for His Glory. Christian joy involves an awareness that whatever happens is happening somehow for the glory of God. Joy adopts the eternal perspective. It sees beyond the present.

Keep Laughing. When asked if she would consider donating a kidney to her sister, the character Sophia of television's *The Golden Girls,* replied, "She wouldn't want it because I can't even control it!" When you cancel your organ donor agreements because everything is either worn out or not working, you know you are getting up there. The incredible human machine, minus a few key cogs, isn't all that incredible.

Remember a sense of humor oils even the loosest frame. One of our friends has multiple sclerosis; another has severe arthritis. They are quite a pair. They joke that when they enter the nursing home, they're going to form the Shake and Ache club.

Our youngest son, Andy, is an organ retrieval expert. He flies all over the Northwest harvesting organs for transplants. We get quite a few jokes out of that profession around our house, as you can imagine. Pearl and I were talking with Andy a few weeks ago about the future of our body parts. Silence speaks volumes...like, "Mom, Dad, who would want them? What have you got left that still works and isn't damaged or repaired?"

Oh well! My body has served me well, and once in a while it even kicks in at full tilt just to let me know I'm not dead yet.

Pearl's vintage 1985 Oldsmobile has 120,000 miles on it and is still running. I'm beginning to understand my affinity for that car. We are a lot alike! The Olds takes more maintenance than a newer model, but it gets you there and back.

Art Linkletter had it right. Laughter is the best medicine. (Being especially intelligent, he also said old age is not for sissies.)

Be Approachable and Affirming. Want to stay joyful? "Let your forebearing spirit be known to all men," Paul wrote the Philippians (4:5). The phrase "forebearing spirit" may also be translated "sweet reasonableness." The term suggests the gentleness of the tongue and conveys the ideas of gentleness, kindness, submissiveness. It is the same word used to describe the wisdom from above in James 3:17.

Approachable, affirming people are sweetly reasonable. They are kind. They arrange to be available. They compromise and do not have to have things their own way. They are sensitive to the needs of others. They are patient. Forebearing spirits put up with a lot. Thank God He's given me several in my life, the most precious of whom is Pearl.

Stop Worrying. All was not well at Philippi. You know they had reason to worry about Paul and Epaphroditus. Were they dead or alive? With Nero the emperor and Epaphroditus so sick, who knew what could happen? Without adequate information it is always easy to believe the worst.

Paul said stop! "Be anxious for nothing" (4:6). The phrase might also be translated: "Stop having anxiety." The Philippians were worrying, so Paul told them to put a sock in it.

Worry involves accepting a responsibility God did not intend us to have. We find ourselves riddled with worry and anxiety when we take our eyes off the Lord and focus on our circumstances. The apostle Peter found that out the hard way. As long as he fixed his gaze upon Jesus, Peter walked atop the waves. One glance at the roiling waters around him and he began to sink. "Help, Lord!" he cried, praying the shortest prayer in Scripture. Jesus pulled him atop the waves again (Matthew 14:27-32).

The bottom line of worry is unbelief. When we worry, we don't believe that God is adequate for the situation. We mistrust His power. We lack faith in His judgment.

Worry agonizes over worst-case scenarios. Ralph Waldo Emerson put it, "Some of your hurts you have cured, and the sharpest you still have survived. But what torrents of grief you endured from evils which never arrived." We can ruin a perfectly good present by worrying about the past and the future.

What do we have to worry about really? I've found that many of the fears of senior adulthood center around health issues, finances, and physical death.

Money is often a concern at retirement when the reality of a permanently reduced income sets in. Chapter twelve deals with financial issues and principles for seniors, so I'll discuss financial concerns there.

But seniors also fear debilitating illness and the future. It is a common misperception that as we retire, our energy and vitality die off and all that survives for a brief, foolish old age is a dry, empty shell. It is unlikely we will be useless in old age unless we were basically useless in pre-retirement days and decide to continue the trend.

We also fear retirement myths, as Horace L. Kerr has suggested. Myth one is that we will die as soon as we retire. We've all heard the story of those who suffered massive coronaries within a few weeks of retirement. Legendary Alabama coach Bear Bryant didn't last long after hanging up his clipboard. I preached a funeral of a man who awoke one day, had coffee, showered, and died. He was sixty-two and until the moment of his death, seemed the picture of health.

Despite such cases, statistics indicate the average senior lives some sixteen years after retirement and there is no difference in the mortality rates of senior workers and retirees of the same age.[6]

A second myth is that senility or mental illness or dementia is imminent once one retires. Not true. Kerr suggests that as little as 5 to 10 percent of those suffering from such diseases are so impaired they cannot function normally. Estimates are that only one-fourth of us will spend time in a long-term care institution like a nursing home.[7] This number is expected to increase, but research in neurological disease is widespread and cures may be found to spare many of us the need for assisted living until we are quite old.

We also fear failure. In retirement we realize that our ground time is brief. We may be disappointed that we haven't accomplished what we wanted to. But failure isn't fatal or permanent. There is still plenty of time.

We are also afraid of death. Is heaven really out there or is it a hoax? The answer is yes, there is a heaven. The personal integrity of the Son of God is on the line.

In Matthew 6:19-34, Jesus told us not to worry. And we don't have that much to worry about. Not really.

CHIGGERS AND MOSQUITOES

There is nothing more uncomfortable than going on a camping trip and being eaten up by chiggers and mosquitoes. The little bloodsuckers can flat take the joy out of an otherwise great experience. Besides, they feast on our most prized possession, the red stuff that keeps us going. Our Boundary Waters canoe expedition to northern Minnesota and southern Canada was an eight-day safari of wonderful memories, but buzzing all around us were thousands of tiny 747s with their landing lights on. Thank goodness we sprayed the runways with OFF.

Life is a lot like that. Worries buzz our strip, but they never land. Not really. Fiery darts and friendly fire shoot at us, but God is faithful. He's been through it before and knows the way home.

My friend Dub loved to tell the story of his daddy, a circuit riding preacher in the Texas Panhandle at the turn of the century. His dad and a companion were caught out in a ripping Texas blizzard. As they rode their horses, they became disoriented in the snowy whiteness. The friend said, "Let the reins loose. The horse knows the way home." Dub's father did so, and the animal led him to safety. Now Dub has found the way safely home, too.

If joy is eclipsed by worry or any of the other things we've discussed, maybe you need to hear 1 Peter 5:7: "Casting all your care on Him because He cares for you." Remember, your Father knows the way home.

ACCEPT THE WAY THE BALL BOUNCES

Notre Dame coach Lou Holtz said, "The man who complains about the way the ball bounces is likely the one who dropped it." The senior who complains about the way the ball bounces in the last stretch is probably the one who dropped it, too, by not planning, searching, seeking, and cultivating joy.

Melinda is married and living independently today because her parents wouldn't quit. Reared in the era before special education classes, Melinda, born mentally retarded, didn't have much of a chance at a normal life. But her folks, Al and Sara, worked and scraped together the money to pay for Melinda's education, and God opened some doors. A successful business venture for Al and Sara. An unexpected opening for Melinda at the state school. God took care of the details. Al and Sara didn't worry. They kept the joy.

You'd think the strain of raising a mentally challenged daughter would have left Al and Sara bitter. Having accomplished so much in life, you'd think they'd be content to kick back in their senior years. No way. Sara, now retired, teaches Sunday school, serves in a Christian ladies guild, helps with a church children's program. They volunteer weekly at our offices to "keep sharp." Mailings, typing, computer work, packing—you name it, the staff saves it for Al and Sara. They have found their joy in Jesus.

In *You Gotta Keep on Dancin'*, Tim Hansel writes of joy. His words are good ones to leave you with:

Joy…is something which defies circumstances and occurs in spite of difficult situations. Whereas happiness is a feeling, joy is an attitude. A posture. A position. A place. As Paul Sailhammer says, "Joy is that deep settled confidence that God is in control of every area of my life."

I have a plaque, sent to me during the most difficult period of my entire life, that says the following:

Tim,
Trust me
I have everything
under control!
Jesus[8]

REFLECTIONS

1. Read Psalm 16:11 and cultivate that personal relationship now.

2. Let the Lord search your heart for joy-robbers. They are likely to increase as the years go by. Don't let them get a toehold.

3. What are you worried about? Get in the habit of handing over your concerns to the One who cares for you.

4. Are you willing to be transparent and vulnerable before the Lord and let Him show you where the joy has gone?

5. Face your fears with the promises of God!

6. Use David's prayer in Psalm 51:12 for yourself: "Restore to me the joy of Thy salvation, and sustain me with a willing spirit."

CHAPTER 11

ON YOUR KNEES

KEEP PRAYING

*I have so much to do, that I cannot get on
without three hours a day of praying.*

MARTIN LUTHER

P rayer, to my teenage sons on nights before big exams,
was a holler for help. (The girls always studied more and
weren't as desperate for divine intervention.)

> Now I lay me down to rest,
> I hope I pass tomorrow's test.
> If I should die before I wake
> That's one less test I have to take.

According to a few wiseacres in our churches, prayer was more
like this anonymous version of the old classic:

> Now I lay me down to sleep,
> The sermon's boring and the subject's deep.
> If I should snore before I wake
> Please poke me, for heaven's sake!

I always hoped they were nodding in agreement, not just
nodding off.

The story is told of an old-timer for whom prayer was an opportunity to bend God's ear with his various aches, pains, ailments, and needs. At the end of the long list of petitions, the old guy added, "Use me, O Lord, use me in Thy work—especially in an advisory capacity."[1]

What exactly is prayer, to you?

Prayer by seniors is sometimes limited to a long list of petitions and requests. Often prayer centers on very valid concerns about health, finances, and family. But as many seniors have discovered, and as the apostle Paul surely knew, genuine, God-honoring prayer is much more than an ongoing wish list faxed skyward. It is more than a cry of desperation when the children are neglectful, the cancer scan positive, the prognosis dim.

Prayer has been called hands-on exploration of uncharted spiritual territory. It is the Christian's vital breath and native air. It brings us close to the heartbeat of God and reveals our need. When offered on behalf of others, it is among the noblest and finest of Christian acts.

In senior adulthood, as perhaps never before, there is the opportunity to achieve the goal of making prayer a habit. No, more than that. A lifestyle.

The great eighteenth-century British evangelist George Whitefield knew the power and importance of prayer. Exhausted from preaching several times one day, he prepared for bed only to be roused by someone who asked him to speak one more time to the crowd which had gathered outside. The weary Whitefield picked up a candle and agreed to preach until the flame died. An hour later, the candle extinguished, Whitefield closed in prayer and retired to his room. The next morning he was found kneeling beside his bed, apparently having passed into eternity while talking with the Father. He literally died on his knees.[2]

Can you think of a better way for a Christian to go? One instant communing with God, the next millisecond ushered directly into His presence?

Whatever happens to us in the homestretch of life, like Whitefield, we will nearly always be able to pray.

"Yeah, and when I'm on my knees," laughed seventy-five-year-old Phil, "I always plan to do several things while I'm down there. I don't want to waste the trip!"

Prayer is never a wasted trip.

Prayer is the means God has provided for us to deepen our relationship with Him by spending time in His presence. Worship, adoration, and praise unclog the channels of joy. As we are transparent and vulnerable, with psalms of repentance on our lips, holes in our fellowship with the Father are stitched shut. We begin to ascertain His heart. Intimacy grows.

Bill Bright of Campus Crusade for Christ has been mightily used by God to draw thousands to Him. He is dedicated to prayer. Co-workers who have traveled with him say they are overwhelmed by the intensity of his commitment to praise God and to pray.

The apostle Paul, restricted in his imprisonment, longed to visit his friends in Philippi (1:26). He couldn't make the journey, but he could pray (1:4,9). In almost all of Paul's epistles, he confessed that he was continually praying for the various churches. His whole life was saturated with communication and communion with God.

WHAT SHOULD I PRAY FOR?

Some say prayer is like a telephone call. Certain folks think they get a busy signal. Some only use prayer for 911 emergencies. Both miss the boat. Prayer is a toll-free number. The freight is paid by the Father and He is waiting to hear from us.

Have you ever wondered what you should pray for? The answer is simple. Everything.

Paul gives a formula for prayer and its promised result in Philippians 4:6-7: "Be anxious for nothing, but in everything by prayer and supplication with thanksgiving let your requests be made known to God. And the peace of God, which surpasses all comprehension, shall guard your hearts and your minds in Christ Jesus."

The advice is easy.

Be anxious for nothing. Don't worry.

Pray for everything. No matter what, pray about it. Nothing is too small or too great for Him.

Do it with thanksgiving. Be grateful.

Whatever your concern or desire, your God is big enough to handle it. "I am the Lord, the God of all mankind. Is anything too hard for me?... Call to me and I will answer you and tell you great and unsearchable things you do not know" (Jeremiah 32:27, 33:3 NIV). "Cast your cares on the Lord and he will sustain you; he will never let the righteous fall" (Psalm 55:22 NIV).

The great preacher G. Campbell Morgan was reportedly asked, "Should a Christian pray about the little things?" To this Morgan is said to have replied, "Can you mention anything in your life that is big to God?" Tidal waves of worry and concern to us are but microscopic ripples to Him.

Jesus said, "Until now you have asked for nothing in My name; ask, and you will receive, that your joy may be made full" (John 16:24). You are free to pray for anything. About anything. For anyone. You are guaranteed to receive an answer that is within the Lord's will and which fits with His greater purpose and plan. You can be assured that He is listening.

Concerned about your grandkids? Pray for them.

Afraid of failure? Pray and read Psalm 32.

Worried about finances? Pray and read Matthew 6:25-34.

Fearful of the future? Pray and read Romans 8:38-39.

At times your prayers may be desperation cries for help, as my friend Bill Lawrence discovered while flying bombing missions in World War II. Bill found it easy to pray—impossible to do much else—as flak from enemy ground forces burst all about him. Psalm 50 says, "Call upon me in the day of trouble; I will deliver you, and you will honor me" (verse 15 NIV). Even today Bill honors God for answering those prayers of long ago.

Prayer clarifies thoughts in times of trouble and decision.

Prayer helps keep us in accord with God's purpose and plan.

Prayer enables us to face the trials of life.

Prayer transforms us.

Prayer empowers victory over the devil, for he trembles when he sees even the weakest saint on his knees.

Prayer facilitates proper responses to the transitions we face as senior adults.

WHAT HAPPENS WHEN I PRAY?

You'll be glad you prayed. Just ask Nehemiah in the Old Testament. When he prayed, God moved mightily, supplying the people and the provision for the rebuilding of Jerusalem. As one of our favorite poets, Ruth Harms Calkin, so appropriately puts it in "The Reason":

God, why am I so often defeated?
Why am I so full of dread and anxiety?
Why am I so lamentably weak—
So perilously susceptible to temptation?
Why am I so often inhospitable
So intolerant of the needs of others?
Why do I protest so violently?
Above all, God
Why do I so frequently lose
The sense of Your shining presence?
God, why?

Why?
"Because you pray so little."[3]

When we fail to pray, we limit ourselves to our own resources. Why settle for the trickle when we can tap into the ocean of God's peace and provision?

Prayer is a privilege for those who are in the family of God through a relationship with Jesus Christ. Romans 5:2 says believers have access to the Father. Flowing from our relationship with the Son comes our prerogative to enter the Father's presence in prayer. We can talk directly to Him!

My wife Pearl is an Anderson by marriage and you can believe she has access to our home (her home) at any time. Like E. F. Hutton, when Pearl speaks, I listen! I cannot imagine locking the door on her or shutting her out. Ridiculous! What a privilege it is to know the Father feels the same. We can have His ear at any time.

Prayer comes with a promised result, wrote the apostle Paul. When we faithfully pray, "the peace of God, which surpasses all comprehension," will guard our "hearts" and "minds" in Christ Jesus (Philippians 4:7).

Hawthorne points out that this verse is the only place in the New Testament where the phrase "the peace of God" is found. Paul is not referring to peace with God, meaning the reconciliation we obtain through faith in Jesus Christ. Nor was he exclusively referring to the inner peace of soul given by God. The "peace of God" is also a peace grounded in God's presence and promise, a direct result of believing prayer.[4]

Sounds simple. We pray. The fruit of peace is born.

The peace of God is more than a fleeting feeling which comes and goes with circumstances. It is based on the Father's assurance that He is there, that He cares, and that He is competent to champion our cause.

Several years ago a company of us gathered at the medical center and prayed around the clock for seventy-two hours that three-year-old Amy Knarr would live. Probably thinking her "floaties" were still on, Amy had rushed from a bathroom at a local lake pool and leaped into the cloudy water before anyone saw her. After a frantic search, her tiny body was discovered at the bottom. Now she lay unconscious in intensive care, but because she had not been underwater long, there was hope of recovery.

We prayed fervently that God would again allow us to hear her bubbly, infectious laughter and see her sparkling smile. One of the ladies praying in the group looked up and said, unexpectedly, "I don't know. I am at peace. I believe God has answered." I felt the same sense. Moments later one of the doctors was calling my name, telling me to go to Dick and Ethel. Amy had just gone home to be with the Lord. Speechless, numb from the tragedy yet still awestruck, every one of us knew that yes, He had answered. A sweeping sense of His presence and peace flooded the room and the hospital corridors. Viewing his little girl's lifeless form, Dick voiced what we all felt, "God, I understand that I don't understand."

This was God's peace.

Paul assures us that when we pray, God's peace will guard our hearts and minds. The phrase might also be translated "hold custody of." Prayer arrests the soul. God's peace pervades our hearts (our feelings and emotions) and our minds (our intellectual processes). Imagine a garrison of soldiers, a small force of men placed inside a fort to hold it against attack while the main body of the army moves to take new ground. Fortification comes from within. God's peace does this for us when we faithfully engage in believing prayer.

Notice, we are not promised that prayer will be answered with the answers we want. God knows better than we what we need. But we are promised peace. "Lord, you establish peace for us; all that we have accomplished you have done for us" (Isaiah 26:12 NIV).

Prayer is simple obedience. Its fruit is a quiet, powerful serenity of heart and mind enabling us to confront all we encounter with Christ's attitude and strength. This goes even for the final laps of life, when losses can be heavy and sorrow may run deep. Nothing, except our own sin of refusing to obey, can hinder believing prayer from reproducing God's peace in our hearts and minds.

POSITIVE PRAYER ATTITUDES

Closeness to God breeds the comfortable ease of free communication with Him. King Saul never learned that truth.

Nowhere in the Old Testament record do we find Saul speaking of the Lord in a personal way. Always with Saul it was "your God," never "my God" or "our God." Not so with the apostle Paul.

Prayer was indispensable to Paul. He knew how to talk to his heavenly Father, and he gave us guidelines for great prayer communication in Philippians 1:3-4: "I thank my God in all my remembrance of you, always offering prayer with joy in my every prayer for you all." I like to call them positive prayer attitudes. They are good principles for us to grab on to.

1. Keep It Up. "Pray without ceasing," Paul recommended elsewhere in Scripture (1 Thessalonians 5:17). I am "always offering prayer with joy" he wrote the Philippians.

Pray always. Let your well never run dry. Your relationship with God is like your marriage or any other important union. When you are firing on all cylinders, intimate communication flows freely. Keep it up.

Besides Paul, when I think of constant prayer, I think of Stonecroft Ministries' Helen Baugh and Mary Clark. These two seniors give fresh meaning to "pray without ceasing." The results of their earnest prayers? Today there are over twenty-two hundred Christian Women's Clubs internationally, where thousands every year hear the gospel of Christ in a non-threatening atmosphere of love and acceptance. There are also more than three hundred village missionaries, trained workers taking the gospel to rural areas and remote locations.

One evening as I prepared to speak at a conference sponsored by Stonecroft, Helen Baugh opened with public prayer. A striking, refined woman in her eighties, she stood at the microphone for several seconds of silence. "God...," her voice resonated throughout the auditorium. Dead silence permeated the assembly. "God," Helen repeated with such choked emotion, reverence, and awe that you knew the Father had put aside everything on His desk and somehow communicated, "Helen, go ahead. I'm ready to hear you." As she continued, we all sensed heaven had come down to that room. In later conversations with staff, I learned that Helen often spends whole nights in prayer. Her life verse is Jeremiah 33:3: "Call to Me, and I will answer you." Thousands are coming to Christ through the work she helped found.

Too old to pray? Nonsense. There is no retirement for prayer warriors. As Solomon prayed, "Even when I am old and gray, do not forsake me, O God" (Psalm 71:18 NIV).

2. Be thankful. Robert Louis Stevenson once said, "The man who has forgotten to be thankful has fallen asleep in life." Let your constant prayers be rich in gratitude and thanksgiving.

Paul instructed the suffering saints in Thessalonica who were so young in the Lord: "In everything give thanks; for this is God's will for you in Christ Jesus" (1 Thessalonians 5:18). Paul thanked God continually for the Philippian believers (1:3). Despite uncertain circumstances, Paul's prayers were full of love and encouragement. He had mastered the attitude of gratitude. Even at the evident end of life, he mirrored the Savior in the upper room: thinking of others, answering their questions, praying for them.

For what and for whom might you give thanks as you pray?

Start out with God Himself. No petition, mind you. Just be with Him. Praise Him for His person, presence, patience. Praise Him for His unconditional love. Thank Him for being who He is and for giving you the power to have victory over temptation and sin. Be overwhelmed by the gifts of His Son and His Spirit! Bubble in His bounty and revel in His resources.

Be thankful for your family—your spouse, kids, grand-children, parents, in-laws!

Be thankful for your country and the freedom you enjoy and the countless thousands who have sacrificed to make it so. Thank God for your home, your health, your host of friends who would come in a minute if you needed anything. Thank Him for your church family and staff and all they do to make your life a joy.

You get the idea.

3. Be Unselfish. Erma Bombeck writes that during a stint in which she spent weeks in Hollywood as executive producer of a television series and came home only on the weekends, she discovered something about marriage she had not appreciated before: "Life isn't much when you no longer have anyone to think about except yourself."[5] Likewise, prayer is more mean-ingful when it isn't just offered on your own behalf!

Paul prayed for the Philippians. They prayed for him. How many folks outside your family and tight circle of friends do you regularly remember in prayer? Intercessory prayer is a hall-mark of the committed Christian life. Be unselfish when you pray. Like Paul, do it for others!

Each morning at eight o'clock our staff meets for thirty minutes to pray for our board of directors and the folks in our classes and camps. Computer printouts serve as guides for each day, so we are sure to cover the needs of those who have entrusted us with their burdens. How exciting it is when peo-ple tell us of God's obvious intervention.

It is an honor to pray for others. Our compassion for people increases as we call upon the Lord. Prayer is itself an act of compassion. The following anonymous poem describes the results:

Was It You Who Prayed?

Did you think of us this morning
As you breathed a word of prayer?
Did you ask for strength to help us
All our heavy burdens bear?
Did you speak of faith and courage,
For the trials we must meet?
Did you ask that God might keep us,
As you bowed at Jesus' feet?
Someone prayed and strength was given
For the long and weary road.
Someone prayed and faith grew stronger,
As we bent beneath our load.
As someone prayed the way grew brighter,
And we walked all unafraid.
In our heart a song of gladness.
Tell us: Was it YOU who prayed?

If you can do nothing else, you can probably pray. Prayer partnership can go all the way to the end of the line. Cindy's mom just went home to be with the Lord after a long struggle with cancer. I know many of her bedridden hours were spent in prayerful intercession for others.

Only the most severely mentally incapacitated are incapable of prayer. Even then, who can know the work of the Holy

218

Spirit within a believer? Before Romans 8:28, "And we know that God causes all things to work together for good," comes Romans 8:26-27: "And in the same way the Spirit also helps our weakness; for we do not know how to pray as we should, but the Spirit Himself intercedes for us with groanings too deep for words; and He who searches the hearts knows what the mind of the Spirit is, because He intercedes for the saints according to the will of God."

God is at work! His Spirit intercedes for us in the very midst of our physical, emotional, and mental afflictions and asks in accordance with the Father's will. When we are weak, even dying, He has our full attention to prepare us for the transition to come!

4. Be joyful. So often the prayers of senior saints center on health concerns (such as upcoming surgeries), financial matters (perhaps real estate to sell), family problems (wayward grandchildren or sons-in-law who aren't good enough for their girls), and matters of personal safety. That's okay. Supplication (asking) is part of prayer. But beware that when you pray, you don't merely fire off some verbose list of requests. Remember you are praying to a friend and Father who loves you more than anyone else is capable of loving you!

Author Barbara Johnson, founder of Spatula Ministries (whose purpose is to scrape hurting people off the ceiling and get 'em going again), keeps a Joy Room as her office. A plaque on the wall reads, "Joy is not the absence of suffering but the presence of God."[6]

"Delight yourself in the Lord and he will give you the desires of your heart," wrote David (Psalm 37:4 NIV). Many take this verse to be a promise of goodies from a celestial Santa Claus or Great Sugar Daddy in the sky. Pray for something hard enough and you'll get it. Trouble is, we hone in on the final part of the verse and forget the first. We latch on to the idea of getting the desires of our heart and conveniently overlook the prerequisite: "Delight yourself in the Lord." As Bing Hunter points out, prayer is a means God uses to give us what He wants, not necessarily what we want.[7] If our joy is in the Lord, our prayers will jibe with His eternal purposes.

God uses prayer to pull us in line with those purposes, too. Paul convinced himself that his ministry would be much more effective if his "thorn in the flesh" were removed. God's answer was no. His grace would instead be sufficient to see Paul through (2 Corinthians 12:8,9).

5. *Remember who is listening.* It was "my God" to whom Paul prayed. When you pray, you aren't talking to empty air or to anyone else in the room. Prayer is conversation between you and God. He is your lover and closest friend.

Don't reduce your conversation with Him to a bunch of gimme's.

Bare your heart with honest confession of how you've blown it. God knows you've sinned. You will experience His forgiveness and restoration of fellowship when you fess up (1 John 1:9). The psalmist wrote, "If I had cherished sin in my heart, the Lord would not have listened" (66:18 NIV). Your prayers won't get beyond the rafters if those conditions aren't met. God is holy.

Come before your Lord with an awesome sense of fear and respect. He loves you, but in His presence you are standing on holy ground.

6. *Be confident in Him.* Finally, when you pray, be confident in God's ability to properly handle your prayers. God

delights in our trust. Paul was "confident" that what he prayed for would come to pass—that God would continue His good work (Philippians 1:6).

SENIOR SUMMITS

We all have time to pray. If you don't think so, review all you've done in the last twenty-four hours. Surely there was a little slack time! Once you get in the habit, and prayer becomes a priority, you won't be concerned about slack time. You'll be consumed with prayer, won't be able to imagine a day without it, and will shove other things aside to do it. It is that life-changing.

Joe Aldrich, President of Multnomah School of the Bible, has authored the challenging book *Prayer Summits*. I recommend it highly. A Prayer Summit is a gathering of pastors or other Christians from the same community for the sole purpose of praying together, reading Scripture, and praising God with songs and hymns. Joe and his team members have sponsored such summits along the West Coast. There is no agenda, no program, just a group of believers of various denominations and backgrounds joining in an extended time (four days) of prayer and praise. After trust is established, the opportunity is offered for those present to share struggles, heartaches, personal needs. Aldrich writes about these moments:

> Only a powerful, sustained time in His presence will tear down ancient walls, build bonds of love, and link brothers in a common cause.
>   When two separated brethren find themselves at the feet of Jesus, at the foot of the same cross, the distance

between them shrinks to almost nothing. As they worship together, weep together, and minister together, things change. Caricatures are eliminated, issues are brought into balance, and hearts are knit in common cause.[8]

Prayer Summits impact individual hearts and whole communities. They are designed for all ages, but after reading Joe's book, I thought of how easy it would be for retired adults to become involved in sponsoring and spreading Summits in their regions.

Whether or not you become involved in a formal work like Prayer Summits, you can still pray. If you don't know what to pray for when interceding for someone else, evangelist Sammy Tippet, crusader for the gospel in Eastern Europe, offers some ideas for those who wish to pray for him and his work:

If God should bring me to mind when you're praying, would you pray that:

I will be like Christ in character and deed.
I will be a Christlike husband and father.
I will be courageous in calling the church to revival.
I will completely depend on God and never on myself.
That I will walk humbly before the Lord and die to self daily.
And that Jesus Christ will be glorified.[9]

Not bad ideas for any of us to incorporate into our prayers, are they? On your knees is a great place to be.

REFLECTIONS

1. Make a commitment right now to find time each day for food from God's Word and fellowship through prayer.

2. Get in the habit of keeping a prayer diary of requests, answers, and praises.

3. Build your personal library with a collection of books on prayer. Try author E. M. Bounds.

4. Make a list of family members, friends, church members, ministers, missionaries, government officials, and other people you want to pray for regularly. Then do it!

5. Set aside time each day simply to praise God—from whom all blessings flow!

6. Don't give up on difficult situations. God is at work.

CHAPTER 12

A WISE INVESTMENT
PLANNING FINANCIALLY
FOR A CHRISTLIKE FINISH

*Any enterprise is built by wise planning,
becomes strong through common sense,
and profits wonderfully by keeping abreast of the facts.*

PROVERBS 24:3,4 TLB

A small ceramic plaque hangs in our kitchen. It reads: "In this house live one beautiful person and one old goat." Pearl bought it in Branson, Missouri, and she didn't say who was who. Our guests never seem to think clarification is necessary either. I guess I'm the only one who figures there might be some doubt. One thing I do know. The story that follows is enough to frighten any old goat.

A farm and ranch magnate was raking in big bucks. Cows were calving and harvests heavy, expansion the name of the game. The windows of bounty were open and he was catching all he could. Limited only by storage capacity, the rich man commissioned plans for additional grain elevators. Once his financial empire was secure, he planned to semi-retire. He intended to leave the management of his assets to others and enjoy the travel, food, and good life afforded him by smart investments and hard work.

Nope. Think again.

In a terrifying nightmare the man heard himself muse on his plans: "And I will say to my soul, 'Soul! You have many goods laid up for many years to come; take your ease, eat, drink and be merry.'" God's answer to the good life thundered through his dream and chilled him to the bone: "You fool! This very night your soul is required of you; and now who will own what you have prepared?" (Luke 12:19-20).

That rich fool had stockpiled wealth only to abruptly discover that you really can't take it with you. King Solomon drew similar conclusions, capturing the irony of having to leave it all to undeserving heirs with this statement: "For a man may do his work with wisdom, knowledge and skill, and then he must leave all he owns to someone who has not worked for it. This too is meaningless and a great misfortune" (Ecclesiastes 2:21 NIV).

The wealthy fool in Jesus' parable lived with botched up priorities. He also neglected to make the proper arrangements for the distribution of his wealth should his money outlast him. God asks, "Who will own what you have prepared?" The government? Your kids? His affairs were not in order, only one of his many mistakes.

Part of achieving a successful senior adulthood means planning so you'll have enough and so some of your money will outlive you. As we'll see, it also means deciding now what to do with whatever money does outlast you.

THE PERKS OF GROWING OLDER

I received a jolt some years back when my AARP card arrived in the mail. I didn't ask for it. And I didn't find it as amusing as my kids did. What I had put off till tomorrow had now become today. I was fifty, and the American Association of Retired Persons had seen fit to log me onto their rolls.

The first time Pearl pulled out her AARP card to see if the desk clerk would give us a discount at a hotel chain, I glared at her. She put it away. "I just thought I'd see if we could save some money," she said in exasperation.

Nowadays I never tell her to put away the AARP card. After a while, clerks and waitresses have you pegged anyway. They know when you qualify for special senior rates—like the gal the other day at breakfast who charged Pearl and me the golden age rate without even asking. Guess it was obvious. (Many workers, it should be noted, have been instructed never to ask customers if they'd like senior discounts. Seems many folks are touchy about their age. Imagine that.)

I've come to appreciate the perks which accompany age. It's about time someone gave our generation a break! As the following excerpt from an anonymous piece called "For All Those Born before 1945" humorously puts it: "We hit the scene when there were 5 and 10 cent stores, where you bought things for five and ten cents. Sanders or Wilson's sold ice cream cones for a nickel or a dime. For one nickel you could ride a street car, make a phone call, buy a Pepsi or even enough stamps to mail one letter and two postcards. You could buy a new Chevy coupe for $600...but who could afford one? A pity, too, because gas was 11 cents a gallon!"[1]

For folks who were born when "Made in Japan" meant junk and AIDS were helpers in the principal's office, the staggering inflation rates of the 1970s and 1980s were shattering. I remember when nice houses sold for less than ten grand and millionaires built truly luxurious mansions for $50,000. Times have changed.

The need to sensibly manage our financial resources has not, especially if our senior years are to be all God would have them to be.

WHAT TO EXPECT WHEN YOU SHUT HER DOWN

One of two things is often true of senior adults. Either they are worried about having enough money on which to live comfortably in retirement, or they are consumed with passing on a legacy to their children and grandchildren. This chapter speaks to both issues.

Before we go further, let me make it clear that I do not claim to be an expert on finances or financial planning. Far from it! I simply hope to provide you with scriptural principles about the use of your assets. Whatever technical information is included comes from reliable sources, and I have depended upon the counsel of Mike Rodgers, a CPA on our staff, and Jerry Reeves, CFO of the Dallas Seminary Foundation, for guidance.

For a far more exhaustive treatment of the financial aspects of senior adulthood, I recommend Larry Burkett's *Preparing for Retirement*. It is an excellent idea to consult a reputable CPA or certified financial planner for advice, too.

Be sure to get references from any "experts" you approach. Investment scams often target seniors. There are many vultures out there who'd like nothing better than to live it up on your money. As a buddy of mine described one such scuzzball, "He's so crooked that when he dies they're going to have to screw him into the ground." There are plenty like that worm. If the deal sounds risky or too good to be true, it probably is.

Don't make the mistake of assuming that just because someone is a Christian, he or she is a sound financial advisor. Be careful. Well-meaning believers can be dead wrong, misled, or misinformed. Many big-time investment opportunities are mishandled by guys who don't have their hardware hooked up right. Their elevator stops a few floors short of the top and you are the loser. If you're not sure about an investment, make like a homesick angel: fly away.

In our marriage, Pearl has always kept me in line financially (and otherwise). I'm the one inclined to say, "Dream with me, baby!" Her response is usually, "Give me reality. You can't take dreams to the bank."

She's right.

Your money is yours and the Lord's, and if you retire, it may have to last a long time. Take care of it.

In dealing with our finances, we must not forget that God promises to provide and is ultimately in control. He also expects us to be good stewards of that which He gives us.

To put it bluntly, you don't want to find yourself on the deck chairs of the Titanic listening to a lecture on icebergs while the ship is taking on water. Now is the time to get ready financially for the homestretch of life and to decide where it's all going when you're gone.

PRE-PLAN YOUR FINANCES

The AARP's guidebook *How to Plan Your Successful Retirement* contains this observation: "Studies show that those who enjoy their retirement most fully have laid careful plans, well in advance, regarding not only finances but also how they will maintain their health in retirement, how they will use their time, and where they will live."[2]

Long before you retire, experts recommend you determine how much income you will need in order to live comfortably.

It may be that you will not be able to retire, but must work full- or part-time to maintain an adequate standard of living. You may discover you'll need to find cheaper housing. The time to uncover this information is long before you get the gold watch and are perhaps forced to make an unexpected move.

As for me, I doubt I will ever retire. I'll continue to write, speak, and teach as long as there are opportunities and health permits. On a recent public radio show commemorating his ninety-eighth birthday, comedian George Burns commented on the secret of his longevity and productivity, "Never retire, and fall in love with what you are doing." I would add as a senior saint, "And stay in love with the One you are knowing!"

YOUR TIME IS VALUABLE...
CAN YOU AFFORD TO GIVE IT AWAY?

If you are able to exit the work force and live on your retirement income, what a boon to many organizations your expertise could be! Some of the happiest seniors I know are those who have arranged their finances so they can give away their time during the golden years.

Henry built a large company, and in his midfifties brought someone else in to assume the leadership as he phased out of his responsibilities. With reduced duties, he was able to become involved in numerous mission trips and evangelical outreaches. He moved neatly from being very active in business to being very active in ministry.

Joe is a successful ophthalmologist who plans to arrange his finances so he can retire early and devote himself to full-time medical missions. The numerous mission trips he has already taken have whetted his appetite, and he looks forward to donating his time meaningfully in senior adulthood.

Fran and Ted heard about the needs of a Christian school in a foreign country. They volunteered to travel there and work for two months doing repair work and various things the school needed. They paid their way, lived modestly in campus housing, and proved very helpful.

Gayelynn and George retired from education and a major corporation, respectively. Now they volunteer three days a week with a Christian organization. Their commitment is not just when it is convenient. They approach the situation as if they were employees and a paycheck depended upon it.

FIVE THREATS TO RETIREMENT INCOME

However seniors choose to spend their time, most hope they'll have few financial worries. The November 1993 issue of *Money* magazine contained the article "Beat the Five Threats to Your Retirement." Author Denise M. Topolnicki listed five areas of concern seniors should address before it's time to retire. I'd like to paraphrase her findings here, but would caution you that federal regulations change almost daily and you should check anything against the most recent information.

1. Pension. Twenty-nine percent of today's retirees collect a private pension, compared with only 9 percent in 1962. Companies are increasingly dropping traditional pensions in favor of cheaper 401(k) plans where employees share the burden of saving for retirement. Investigate your company's pension plan, if any. Defined-contribution plans such as the 401(k) depend upon how much you invest in them. Your company then makes contributions proportionate to what you have made. If you don't save much in this type of plan, you can't expect much of a pension![3]

If you are fortunate enough to have a traditional pension which your company funds, just how much monthly income can you expect? Is it secure? Is it insured? (Often companies "borrow" from retirement accounts in financial crunches. Don't expect that the pension you've been promised will necessarily be what you get.) Do you have the option of taking a lump sum at retirement? What, if any, benefits will you retain after leaving the company? Will your spouse have survivorship rights to your pension income in the event of your death? What will the payout be in that case?

2. *Health care.* Soaring medical costs can cut into the fattest retirement purse. Observed Topolnicki, "Today only a third of all retirees get low- or no-cost health insurance from their former employers, and that figure is getting sucked south."[4]

Medicare, the government-insured health care program, kicks in at sixty-five, but it does not cover all health-care costs. If you are unable to obtain coverage from your former employer, investigate purchasing a supplemental insurance (Medigap) policy to help cover the 20 percent (as of 1994) Medicare does not. Realize that Medicare will not pay for all medical procedures and will only pay standard amounts for other procedures. Your doctor may charge more than the program will pay.

Something else to consider: Nursing home costs are not covered by most insurance policies, including Medicare, unless skilled nursing care is required. Even then, the number of covered days in a nursing home is limited. With an annual price tag of fifteen thousand dollars to thirty thousand dollars, an extended nursing home stay can wipe out a nest egg pronto.

Medigap supplemental insurance policies cost anywhere from three hundred dollars to three thousand dollars per year. If you choose early retirement, remember you won't be eligible for Medicare until age sixty-five, and private health insurance costs are exorbitant. The federal COBRA law generally entitles you to purchase insurance at your or your spouse's former employer's group rate for eighteen months. By waiting till you are at least six months past your sixty-third birthday to retire, you may save a bundle.[5]

3. *Social Security.* Check out your Social Security benefits, too. Social Security is only a supplement to retirement income and will not be enough for you to live on. As we have discussed, it will likely be reduced even further as the baby boom generation ages. In the past year, Congress has authorized increased taxation of Social Security income. Count on fewer benefits.

4. *Inflation.* "Even at a gentle 3% a year, inflation cuts the value of a traditional pension in half in 23 years," noted Topolnicki. Pension plans often do not come with cost-of- living increases. Inflation can stunt the growth of retirement savings if you have too much rolled into fixed-income investments.[6]

5. *Yourself.* Topolnicki's article suggests that often the greatest threat to retirement income is the one expecting to retire. We sabotage ourselves by failing to adequately save. The Japanese save at three times our national rate; the Germans, double. Topolnicki suggests that we "stop living only for today" and make lifetime commitments to saving significantly and funding retirement plans to the max.[7]

A WORD ON CONTENTMENT

One thing articles like the one in *Money* don't usually mention: sometimes less is more. There are benefits to lightening the load.

In the classic *The Wizard of Oz*, the Scarecrow wanted a brain; the Lion, courage; the Tin Man, a heart. Dorothy just wanted Kansas. With all the supposed power of the incredible Oz at their feet, these four friends made surprisingly simple requests. When you get down to it, we really don't need all that much, do we?

This was a secret learned by the apostle Paul, who wrote the Philippians that he had "learned to be content," no matter what the circumstances (4:11). The word translated "content" is an expression borrowed from the Stoics and conveys the idea of self-sufficiency. Paul isn't suggesting that he is independent of God; he is independent of circumstances! He is untroubled by the externals. His happiness doesn't depend on how much he has or how comfortable he is. His contentment isn't based upon people or things.

Like Paul, may we discover that we don't need all that much. And may we never forget that God expects us to be good stewards of what we do have.

DO YOUR GIVING WHILE YOU'RE LIVING, THEN YOU'RE KNOWING WHERE IT'S GOING

Jesus concluded His powerful Sermon on the Mount with a little story. Two guys were drawing up house plans. One chose a rock as his building site. Maybe he liked the view. The other chose to build on the sand. He wanted to be near the surf. When the rains descended and the floods came and the winds blew and burst against the two houses, the one built upon the rock rode out the storm intact. The one on the sand took the same shots, and as Mother Nature huffed and puffed, she blew the house down. Great was the fall.

According to pastor Tony Evans, the moral of this story is that it's going to rain...and when it does, it's too late to pour concrete.

It's inevitable that one day the storm will rain on us. Our time on earth will be finished. When that moment arrives, we may find ourselves greatly concerned about the Father's "What have you done?" list. On that list, I believe the first question will be: What have you done with My Son? Somewhere down the line will be this question: What have you done with the funds? Where has all the money gone?

There is a flip side to the fiscal concerns of senior adulthood. We are exhorted in Scripture directly and by example to give of our financial resources (2 Corinthians 8:1-5). Before the rest of our life is over, we must deal with the issue of what will happen to all we have accumulated.

Generous giving is scriptural. Many seniors believe they just don't have enough to give, but even a small portion of a fixed income honors God when it is given freely and cheerfully. The widow at Zarephath shared her meager bit of oil and flour with the prophet Elijah, and God faithfully cared for her needs by keeping up the supply during the crisis (2 Kings 17:7-16). It was another widow's mite that moved the Lord Jesus to commend her (Luke 21:1-4).

My mother lives on a very limited income, but her gifts to the Lord's work are made on schedule each month. She's living out a principle stated in Proverbs: "Honor the Lord with your wealth, with the firstfruits of all your crops; then your barns will be filled to overflowing, and your vats will brim over with new wine" (Proverbs 3:9-10 NIV).

Wealthy seniors face different challenges. It can be too easy for them to get what they want, go where they want, do what they want. As Auren Uris pointed out, "But when the whole world's your oyster, one more pearl doesn't mean all that much."[8] Money sometimes only purchases boredom. Physical luxuries become emotional necessities, and concepts of money and its function are skewed. A relentless pursuit of the things of this earth never brings happiness.

As amazing as it sounds, many times wealthy Christians give less to Christ's work than relatively poor ones. It is not at all unusual for seniors on modest incomes to proportionately out-give their wealthier contemporaries. I know a man who is a millionaire many times over. He considers giving fifty dollars a sacrifice. Another is working long past the age of retirement just so he will have discretionary income to give generously. Like so many with little of the world's goods, he is unbelievably openhanded.

When determining the direction of your finances, I recommend meditating on 2 Corinthians 9:6-8: "Now this I say, he who sows sparingly shall also reap sparingly; and he who sows bountifully shall also reap bountifully. Let each do just as he has purposed in his heart; not grudgingly or under compulsion, for God loves a cheerful giver. And God is able to make all grace abound to you, that always having all sufficiency in everything, you may have an abundance for every good deed."

The great thing about these verses is you can choose the size of your crop. It's your call! In matters of giving, we are to do what we decide to do in our hearts. God appreciates the attitude, "Oh, boy, I get to give!" rather than "Do I have to?" God loves a cheerful—literally a hilarious—giver. After all, He's one, too!

YOU'LL BE GLAD YOU GAVE

Paul's letter to the Philippians is partly a thank-you note. We read in Philippians 4 that Epaphroditus had taken a monetary gift to Paul from Philippi. The apostle was grateful.

This wasn't the first time Paul's friends at Philippi had been so generous with his ministry. In the early days, not one church gave even a dime (make that a drachma) to Paul's ministry, except the Philippians (4:15). Not only did they support him while he was in Rome and in their midst, they also contributed to Paul's work elsewhere: "For even in Thessalonica you sent a gift more than once for my needs" (4:16). Notice: they sent more than one gift to Thessalonica...and the apostle was probably only there about three weeks! In his letter, Paul reminded the Philippians of this, encouraging and praising them.

It wasn't so much the money that mattered to Paul as it was that the Philippians would reap eternal rewards because of their right-minded generosity. The Father's heavenly computer was recording the transaction. God knew their generosity. What the Philippians had sent by Epaphroditus was "a fragrant aroma, an acceptable sacrifice, well-pleasing to God" (4:18).

The Philippians understood the importance of the counsel given by the writer of Hebrews: "And do not neglect doing good and sharing; for with such sacrifices God is pleased" (Hebrews 13:16). God is the ultimate giver. He values giving in His children. Romans 12:1 calls for us to give our bodies as tools for His use and service. The Philippians were called upon to give of their meager means, and they did so unreservedly.

The sacrifices of the believer which please God are three-fold: 1. The sacrifice of our blessings—what comes from our lips in honor of God, the praises we utter in response to our relationship with Him. 2. The sacrifice of our bodies—making our hands, feet, minds, our very lives available to the Lord to do with what He wants. 3. The sacrifice of belongings—giving our possessions, money, material goods for His service.

When we are generous, God provides. As Paul put it in Philippians 4:19, "And my God shall provide all your needs according to His riches in glory in Christ Jesus."

It is a scriptural principle that as we faithfully provide for others, God faithfully provides for us:

> One man gives freely, yet gains even more; another withholds unduly, but comes to poverty. A generous man will prosper; he who refreshes others will himself be refreshed (Proverbs 11:24-25 NIV).

> Cast your bread upon the waters, for after many days you will find it again (Ecclesiastes 11:1 NIV).

It's all His anyway. Why not let Him worry about distributing the wealth? But you've got to be willing to let go. Open those chubby hands and turn your toys over to Him.

THE SACRIFICE OF OUR BELONGINGS

As we approach our last years, we are in the unique position of deciding how the fruits of our earthly labors will be used when we no longer need them.

The article "A Generation Prepares To Transfer Its Trillions" in the November 16, 1993, issue of *The Chronicle of Philanthropy* reports that a staggering ten trillion dollars is expected to pass from one American generation to the next over the decades to come, resulting in the "largest transfer of wealth in the nation's history."[9] Whatever part of these trillions is comprised of your assets, you have some decisions to make.

What will happen to your money when you are gone?

Of course, if an extended illness requires extensive hospitalization and nursing home care, you may not have as much to dispose of as you thought you would. Exorbitant health care costs take a chunk out of many retirement funds.

But what do you do with what's left?

Many seniors plan to leave substantial legacies to their kids and grandkids. They fail to reckon with the tax penalties such generosity may incur. They sometimes fail to fully think through the effect their well-meaning generosity may have on the next generation. They may ignore opportunities to further God's work with their money.

Depending upon the net worth of your estate, it is possible to more than adequately take care of your descendants while also putting your money to work for the Lord through charitable giving. Many committed Christian seniors are planning to care for both family and the Lord's work. Why not think about being generous with ministries and charities, as well as family, when you plan your estate?

SHOULD I GIVE IT ALL TO THE KIDS?

This is a question many seniors wrestle with. Leaving large sums of money to your children sometimes has the effect of buying them a winning lottery ticket. Like the prodigal son, they may use it up on short-term pleasures and when it is exhausted, they are none the better. Occasionally I have seen that with the departure of funds, goes the remembrance of the benefactor.

Sometimes having too much discretionary income causes staggering financial problems for young folks. Tax penalties, investments turned sour—money can cause trouble if you are not mature enough to handle it. There is something to be said for allowing your kids to make their own way, too. I doubt we help our children when we deny them the pleasure of earning and making that last mortgage or car payment! There is satisfaction in retiring your own debts.

Pearl and I are planning to skip a generation in our estate planning so our funds will be used to help our grandchildren pursue college educations. We'll do this, that is, if there is anything left after we're gone. Sometimes I think finishing well means simply breaking even.

The words of Jesus in the Sermon on the Mount are worth considering here: "Do not lay up for yourselves treasures upon earth where moth and rust destroy, and where thieves break in and steal, but lay up for yourselves treasures in heaven, where neither moth nor rust destroy, and where thieves do not break in or steal, for where your treasure is, there will your heart be also" (Matthew 6:19-21).

When you leave it all for the kids to consume, they may disappoint you, and the eternal possibilities that your money might have accomplished may go down the drain. I am convinced that part of laying up treasure for yourself in heaven means creating a plan whereby you leave a legacy for Christ that keeps producing long after you are gone.

DALLAS SEMINARY FOUNDATION

One organization dedicated to helping men and women plan their estate giving while minimizing tax liability is the

Dallas Seminary Foundation. The Foundation (DSF) was created in 1987 to assist evangelical Christians wishing to invest in the Lord's work.

Millions of dollars are lost to estate and income taxes each year as individuals sell businesses or appreciated assets or plan their estates. The law provides tools for reducing taxes while providing for family and giving to charity, and the folks at DSF help clients plan accordingly. DSF is a ministry of Dallas Theological Seminary and no fees are charged for consultations. Nor do gifts have to be directed to the seminary.

Jerry Reeves, CFO of the Foundation, calls estate planning "the largest financial decision most people make." Reeves, along with financial planners, accountants, and estate planning experts, has compiled a presentation detailing the major choices one faces in disposing of wealth. With his permission, I'd like to summarize some of the foundation's main points.

ESTATE PLANNING CHOICES

When you and your spouse pass on, who receives your estate? 1. Your children and other family members. 2. The government through taxes. 3. Whatever charities you specify. That's it! DSF recommends asking the following questions concerning each recipient:

Children: What is best?
Taxes: What is required?
Charities: What is pleasing to the Lord?

Children—What Is Best? The world's view is that the more money one has, the better off he or she is. DSF recommends that the giving of an inheritance should be thoughtfully weighed before the Lord. Do you opt to leave nothing for your children? If your estate is large enough, would you like to provide for their basic needs in the future? Do you want to do more—perhaps give them a good start in life or provide for major needs? Do you want them to have an abundance, perhaps never to have to work?

What consequences will your decision have? Will your children be resented by their peers or unable to relate to others in their age group who must struggle financially? Will they be able to handle abundance? How spiritually mature are they? Are they walking with the Lord? Do they have a clear sense of purpose? Are they interested in and able to manage money? Are they emotionally mature and stable? Are they generous?

What effect will your bequest have upon their marriage and lifestyle? Do you want to wait till you die to distribute your money, or would you like to see the kids and grandkids enjoy it now?

One individual assisted by DSF has the ability to provide a substantial inheritance to his children but feels this would not be beneficial to them. He has arranged his estate plan so that his kids will receive a certain level of income for a few years, then receive a modest inheritance a few years later. A few years after this, the children will receive a final, relatively modest inheritance.

The man's rationale is to provide his children with some income to help them become established, then some additional funds to manage. After they have experience with this, additional funds will come. Beyond this minimal help, he wants his children to be able to make it on their own. The bulk of his large estate will go to charity, and thanks to preplanning for this, his estate taxes have been greatly reduced, and more is available for nonprofit organizations.

One couple opted to give as much as they could tax-free to their children, then earmarked the rest of their estate for charity, thereby avoiding heavy tax penalties.

Another couple's children were very oriented toward Christian ministry and actually encouraged their parents to develop a plan in which the entire estate would be given to churches and ministries. Both children were doing reasonably well in their careers and believed it would be good for their parents to give it all away when they passed on.

Taxes—What Is Required? As the old saying goes, death and taxes are unavoidable and, for most people, are about equally pleasurable. I hear one fellow was so frustrated with the government's drain on his income that he instructed his family to have his body cremated at death and to send the ashes to Washington, D.C., with the following message: "Now you have it all!"

Today, at least, the government doesn't really have to get it all. Basically (and the rules change all the time), any amount left to a surviving spouse is tax-free. Bequests to charity are tax-free. With proper planning, a total of six hundred thousand dollars apiece may be given to individuals tax-free. After the six hundred thousand dollars, for each dollar given to an individual, approximately one dollar is owed in taxes. Life insurance benefits usually pass to heirs tax-free.

There are legal ways of reducing this tax liability. DSF specializes in helping men and women redirect their planning so that taxes are less, the family gets as much as the parents wish, and charities receive that which might otherwise have been lost to taxes. I was amazed as Jerry Reeves explained that by increasing the charitable giving in an estate plan, the amount going to taxes can be significantly reduced. It is possible for the children to receive a large, well-planned inheritance, while charities also receive large amounts and the government gets less.

One couple wants to benefit their children and grandchildren at a reasonable, yet fairly modest, level compared to what they could do. Their plan is to give to their children and grandchildren while they are living, making sure that the amounts are below the taxable level. They are also gifting many Christian ministries and charities. Their desire is not to have very much in their estate by the time they pass away.

Charity—What Is Pleasing to the Lord? This is a matter between you and God. If you decide God is leading you to give a generous portion of your assets to a ministry or charity, DSF suggests you ask two questions:

1. Why is this ministry a good place to make a significant investment?
2. How would the funds be used?

As one couple phased into retirement, they decided to sell one of their businesses. The money was placed in a charitable trust so that capital gains taxes could be avoided. The funds are available to be given to charities and ministries as the people see fit. This "giving fund" has already greatly benefitted many organizations.

Sometimes it isn't the money we have but certain possessions which can be turned over to God's work. One widow realized that the lake house she and her husband had owned for many years was seldom used after his death. The children were grown and away from home, and the upkeep of the additional house was something she didn't care to continue. Rather than simply selling the home and paying taxes on the profits, she donated the home to a Christian ministry. The widow received a sizeable income tax deduction, and the ministry was able to sell the property and benefit from the proceeds.

The possibilities are limitless. Your church would surely make use of a significant gift. Colleges and seminaries depend upon the generosity of donors. Christian organizations look to God's people in faith for support. As our own ministry is in the process of developing a Christian adult retreat center in central Texas, I know we are greatly encouraged by the generosity of men and women who are joining us to leave this legacy which will minister to marriages and families long after we are gone.

YOU CAN'T TAKE IT WITH YOU

Whatever you decide, with the Lord, about the distribution of your estate, remember that anything you give to Him and His work is a wise investment. Consider it carefully. Plan it now.

Remember, too, that great riches do not guarantee happiness. At a reader's request, Ann Landers recently reprinted the following letter which first appeared in her column in 1989:

Dear Ann:
This is for the folks who believe that money and power open a magic door to happiness. Look what happened to:
1. A man who was head of one of the world's greatest monopolies.

2. A man who was one of the most successful speculators on Wall Street.

3. The former president of the largest independent steel company in America.

4. Past chairman of one of the country's largest utility companies.

5. A former president of the largest gas company in the United States.

6. A man who was once the president of the New York Stock Exchange.

7. A former president of the Bank of International Settlements.

8. A man who was a member of President Harding's Cabinet.

Here are the names that go with the "happenings."

Ivar Krueger, head of International Match Corp. (known as the "match king"), died a suicide—or was murdered. The truth was never established.

Jesse Livermore, the "most wondrous of the 'boy wonders'" of Wall Street, died a suicide.

Charles M. Schwab, chairman of Bethlehem Steel, died broke.

Samuel Insull, chairman of Commonwealth Edison Company and other utility corporations, was acquitted on embezzlement and mail-fraud charges. He died in Paris in modest surroundings.

Howard Hopson, president of the Associated Gas and Electric Utility empire, had been in prison for mail-fraud charges and died in a sanitarium.

Richard Whitney, president of the New York Stock Exchange, served time in Sing Sing for grand larceny.

Leon Fraser, president of the World Bank for International Settlements, died a suicide.

Albert Fall, secretary of the interior in Harding's Cabinet, served a prison term for accepting a bribe.[10]

Money doesn't buy health, longevity, happiness...or what it did last year. Consider seriously what effect your last financial statement will have on the future.

REFLECTIONS

1. Develop a budget you can live with now that includes saving for the future.

2. Choose organizations and missionaries you endorse.

3. Plan now so that you'll be able to give away some of your time and talents to worthwhile causes later.

4. Take the advice God gave Hezekiah (Isaiah 38:1). Put your affairs in order now. Make the tough decisions about what will be done with your estate so that someone else doesn't end up making those decisions.

5. Look realistically at your estate and your family. What will be best for the children? Required by the government? Right before the Lord?

6. Share your vision and passion with your family. The reading of the will is no place for surprises.

CHAPTER 13

LEARNING TO LEAN
DEPENDING ON
THE ADEQUACY OF CHRIST

🖜

For this God is our God for ever and ever;
he will be our guide even to the end.

PSALM 48:14 NIV

I think we have a special seat for you," said the reservations clerk with a grin. My eighty-five-year-old mother, by no means a frequent flyer, gratefully accepted the upgrade to first class. It was only right. First class is where she belongs.

During Dad's extended illness, my sister helped Mom sort through the confusing mass of insurance forms, hospital records, and doctors' statements. When Dad died, we wondered how Mom would cope. She didn't even have a driver's license! Dad had paid all the bills, written all the checks, taken Mom to the grocery store. What would she do?

Let me tell you, what she has done is fine. We needn't have worried. She has stayed active and useful and learned to manage her affairs quite nicely. What an example! "I thought it was time to go see Daddy," she remarked after a recent bad spell. Not yet, Mom. We need you here.

Mike Rodgers of our staff has an eighty-six-year-old grandmother named Dortha who keeps a record of the pies she makes each year for church and neighborhood functions. In

1993 the count was more than her age. After nursing a termi- nally ill husband, making his last months as comfortable as she could, Dortha shifted gears. For years she managed the church kitchen and coordinated activities in her mobile home com- munity. In her early eighties, the kitchen job became a bit too much, so she cut back and became a consultant. They consult her still! If you need a meal for 150, Dortha can do it. The mobile home park keeps hopping because she initiates and organizes activities and services.

Jo, widowed in her late sixties, signed up for Bible Study Fellowship's five-year course the fall after her husband died. Now she's on her last semester. In her spare time she serves at church and volunteers with Child Evangelism Fellowship and a local hospital. She shows no sign of slowing down.

These three women have much in common. All have known grief and endured the heartache of nursing a loved one who did not recover. Each has had to spend significant retire- ment years alone. And all are believers who have learned that God's power is sufficient, His grace generous, and His strength able to sustain their weaknesses.

Cliff knew it, too. I'll never forget when they wheeled him into the hospital for the last time. He had suffered a long, painful illness with many crises and setbacks. That last time Cliff looked at me and said, "I think we are getting close!" How right he was.

THE STRONGER FOR THE WEAK

Facing the reality of human tragedy, we tend to think we can't cope, even as Christians. We don't believe we could handle the death of a spouse or child, the debilitating illness of a loved one, the ravages of a disease of our own, the trauma of losing everything we have, the shame of being forced to sell our possessions, the indignity of depending on our children for support. We think we couldn't do it. We wouldn't survive. Any such trial would be the death of us. And it might.

But you know, it probably wouldn't.

We would survive.

And some of us would survive better. Without becoming bitter. Without resisting. Without kicking. Without resenting. With great, great joy. We would achieve this soaring survival not because of the kind of people we are, but because of the one person we do know: the God who gives us His strength to compensate for our weaknesses. We'd make it, thanks to Him. Better yet, we'd go to be with Him in His time. God hasn't lost a battle or a believer yet.

Compensation of the stronger for the weaker is a principle of life. The two-hundred-ninety-pound lineman always blocks for the running back and defends the quarterback. Big brother is supposed to watch out for little sis as they walk to school. (The operative word is *supposed.* If you have kids, you know what I mean.)

It is God who arms us with strength and makes our way perfect (2 Samuel 22:33). As we declare our dependence upon the Designer, He gives us His power to overcome obstacles, to undergo tests, to navigate turbulent waters, and most of all, to finish this life as winners.

LEARN TO LEAN

The closer I get to the tape, the more I want my finish to be a good one. Please, Lord, let me cross the line and fall into your arms! And with each passing year, I realize that going out in a blaze of glory involves learning to lean now. We cannot go it alone.

"I couldn't go through what she is going through," you find yourself saying when viewing the struggle of a dear friend. Oh yes, you could. Not by yourself of course—but by appropriating the strength and power, resources and protection available to you through Jesus Christ our Lord. And you will do so if you are serious about your walk with the Lord, if you want to accomplish more spiritually than just going through the motions. Paul longed to know Christ "and the *power* of his resurrection and the fellowship of his sufferings, being conformed to his death" (3:10, italics mine).

In the Old Testament, Samson knew what it was to have God's strength surging through him so that he could do that which otherwise would have been impossible.

The Scriptures are filled with examples and promises of God's strength and power. His resources are there, waiting for his children to make use of them:

He was there for David:

It is God who arms me with strength and makes my way perfect (2 Samuel 22:33 NIV).

For Elisha and his servant:

When the servant of the man of God got up and went out early the next morning, an army with horses and chariots had surrounded the city. "Oh, my lord, what shall we do?" the servant asked.

"Don't be afraid," the prophet answered. "Those who are with us are more than those who are with them."

And Elisha prayed, "O Lord, open his eyes so he may see." Then the Lord opened the servant's eyes, and he looked and saw the hills full of horses and chariots of fire all around Elisha (2 Kings 6:15-17 NIV).

For Jehoshaphat:

O Lord, God of our fathers, are you not the God who is in heaven? You rule over all the kingdoms of the nations. Power and might are in your hand, and no one can withstand you....

O our God, will you not judge them? For we have no power to face this vast army that is attacking us. We do not know what to do, but our eyes are upon you....

He said, "Listen, King Jehoshaphat and all who live in Judah and Jerusalem! This is what the Lord says to you: 'Do not be afraid or discouraged because of this vast army. For the battle is not yours, but God's'"
(2 Chronicles 20:6,12,15 NIV).

For Peter in the garden...and waiting in the wings for the Lord Jesus Himself:

And behold, one of those who were with Jesus reached and drew out his sword, and struck the slave of the high priest, and cut off his ear.

Then Jesus said to him, "Put your sword back into its place; for all those who take up the sword shall perish by the sword.

"Or do you think that I cannot appeal to My Father, and He will at once put at My disposal more than twelve legions of angels" (Matthew 26:51-53).

For you and for me:

Come to me, all who are weary and heavy-laden, and I will give you rest. Take My yoke upon you, and learn from Me, for I am gentle and humble in heart; and you shall find rest for your souls. For My yoke is easy, and My load is light (Mt. 11:28-30).

APPROPRIATE HIS STRENGTH

You don't have the strength? Oh yes you do, if you know the Lord Jesus as Savior and if you are availing yourself of what He offers through His Spirit. "For God has not given us a spirit of timidity, but of power and love and discipline" (2 Timothy 1:7). Appropriating His strength should be a tangible goal of retirement. There is no better way to go out than by learning to lean on God.

Paul wrote to Timothy, "I thank Christ Jesus our Lord, who has strengthened me, because He considered me faithful, putting me into service" (1 Timothy 1:12). He echoed this message in Philippians 4:13, "I can do all things through Him who strengthens me."

Who made Paul strong? None other than Jesus Christ. The strength came in "all things," too—meaning every situation Paul had ever faced. As another has said, "The task ahead is not greater than the power behind." How true, when that power is Jesus Christ.

We must not pray for life to be easier, but for God to make us stronger. We must not pray for tasks equal to our might, but for God-given might equal to our tasks. With Paul, we must learn that God's grace is sufficient, and His power is perfected in our weakness. "Therefore I am well content with weaknesses, with insults, with distresses, with persecutions, with difficulties, for Christ's sake; for when I am weak, then I am strong" (2 Corinthians 12:10).

What a glorious realization to know that as we grow weaker and weaker, God's strength can be more radiantly displayed in us. He is there, He cares, and He will supply us with what it takes to cope, that we might be "strengthened with all power, according to His glorious might, for the attaining of all stead-fastness and patience, joyously" (Colossians 1:11).

It is electrifying to understand that we have a source of strength outside ourselves to empower us to handle what lies ahead, even the bumps and bruises:

> Do you not know?
>   Have you not heard?
> The Lord is the everlasting God,
>   the Creator of the ends of the earth.
> He will not grow tired or weary,
>   and his understanding no one can fathom.
> He gives strength to the weary
>   and increases the power of the weak.
> Even youths grow tired and weary,
>   and young men stumble and fall;
> but those who hope in the Lord
>   will renew their strength.

They will soar on wings of eagles;
   they will run and not grow weary,
   they will walk and not be faint
            (Isaiah 40:28-31 NIV).

Paul had strength for all things—the flying, the running, the walking, the prevailing. In life or death, in prison or free, when full or hungry, in plenty or want—God's strength sustained him. The wonderful power of the indwelling Christ enabled him to do anything that was in the mind of God for him to accomplish.

Like Paul, the person who walks with Christ and lives with Christ can do anything Christ has for that person to do: "Not that we are adequate in ourselves to consider anything as coming from ourselves, but our adequacy is from God" (2 Corinthians 3:5).

There may be no better example of one who appropriated God's strength in old age than the Old Testament hero Caleb. Good name, Caleb. It means, literally, "dog," and suggests steadfastness, faithfulness, and good old gutsy courage. Caleb had all of these qualities and more, including a solid dependence upon the Lord to see him through.

Caleb sided with Joshua against ten other members of the committee who voted no to entry into the Promised Land. The majority ruled. Forty-five years later, Caleb was as ready as he was on the day he was outvoted. "I am still as strong today as the day Moses sent me out; I'm just as vigorous to go out to battle now as I was then" (Joshua 14:11 NIV). When he made that statement, Caleb was in his eighties. His strength could have come from nowhere but the Lord! What a tremendous picture of an old man wholly following God, and drawing his power straight from the source.

Like Caleb, as we face the last laps of life, how much we need to remember Christ's presence, power, permission, and position. In other words, whatever we confront, let's remember:

1. The Lord is *alive.*
2. He is *adequate.*
3. He has *allowed* it.
4. He is *available* to carry us through it.

In the words of the hymnist:

He giveth more grace when the burdens grow greater;
He sendeth more strength when the labors increase.
To added affliction He addeth His mercy;
To multiplied trials, His multiplied peace.

When we have exhausted our store of endurance,
When our strength has failed ere the day is half done,
When we reach the end of our hoarded resources,
Our Father's full giving has only begun.

His love has no limit; His grace has no measure;
His pow'r has no boundary known unto men.
For out of His infinite riches in Jesus,
He giveth, and giveth, and giveth again![1]

TURN-TRUST-TRIUMPH

The secret of letting God give His strength to us is simply to avail ourselves of it. We need not wait for an offer of provision. It has already been made. Immediately when the storm hits, and it will, we have the option of following the three T's:

1. *Turn to Him.* Our level of spiritual maturity can often be measured by how long it takes us to turn to God from the time a crisis strikes. The quicker we lean, the more mature we are. Rapid turning means we've learned from experience that He's going to have to handle it anyway. The sooner the better. When we insist on doing things our way, without the Lord, we get our lives so tangled in granny knots and backlashes that the unwinding takes twice the time. Better to turn, fast.

2. *Trust Him.* Once we turn to Him and ask the Lord to handle a situation, we've got to trust Him to do it. There's no sense picking it back up again—for that is nothing more than turning away. Trust means we depend. We have faith that He will show us what to do and give us strength to do it.

We need to act like our old cat, Toodles. A stray picked up by our daughter Becky at a conference ground where Pearl and I served, Toodles lived with us for many years. In her lengthy life, she was run over, smashed under the garage door, and subjected to the indignities of life with a dog. Yet Toodles always bounced back. She trusted me totally. I wouldn't be surprised if she said to herself daily, "He loves me. He feeds me. He wants what's best for me. I'm hanging in with him." And she did, till the inevitable day when Pearl and I became petless.

God would like to see similar responses of trust from us. He loves us. He cares for us. He wants what's best for us. We might as well hang in with Him! And that means trust.

3. *Triumph.* This comes from turning and trusting. It is the inevitable outcome of any crisis, if our response has been

Christ-centered. We will know triumph. Paul put it this way, "But thanks be to God, who always leads us in His triumph in Christ, and manifests through us the sweet aroma of the knowledge of Him in every place" (2 Corinthians 2:14).

Lately these lessons of turning, trusting, and triumphing have come home for me. I've found God often likes to work out principles in my life before he uses me to teach them to others. Sometimes it hurts. This one did.

I've mentioned already that hip replacement surgery has made me attuned to the physical deterioration of aging. What I didn't discuss was the surprise our former insurance company handed us three months before surgery. I was dreading the operation enough, but to make matters more interesting, we received notice that our monthly premiums were going to escalate dramatically and that the change would be immediate.

From approximately one thousand dollars per month, we would be required to pay over four thousand. Ouch! That was quite a sizeable increase, far above anything we ever expected or budgeted for. We couldn't change insurance companies until after my costly surgery, either. We were stuck between the proverbial rock and a hard place.

What could we do? We had only one option: Turn, Trust, Triumph. In the process of turning, we fired off letters to the men who serve on our board and so faithfully provide wise counsel and guidance for our ministry. They are the decision-makers and we are accountable to them. The board and our entire staff then commenced to pray. *En masse* we turned the situation over to the Lord. We did our homework and research, mind you. We wanted to be looking so we wouldn't miss an answer He might show. But the problem was His. So we trusted.

Guess what? He enabled us to triumph! No, the insurance company didn't miraculously change its mind…and by the way, we now purchase insurance from another firm. God gave the triumph by supplying the exorbitant need.

The answer came in the mail in the form of three separate donations for three unusually large amounts from three sources who could not possibly have known about our crisis because we do not publicize such things. For the Lord's work, done the Lord's way, the Lord will provide. And so He did, triumphantly.

Score: Trouble 0, God 1.

GOING OUT IN A BLAZE OF GLORY

The snow had been falling all weekend, transforming the pine-covered landscape into a white-blanketed Christmas card scene. The college ski retreat at The Firs Chalet had been successful. Dr. V. Raymond Edman had been the speaker for the weekend, and lives had been touched for eternity.

Riding next to Dr. Edman on the bus down the winding Mt. Baker road was a rare treat. Captivated by the Father's handiwork at every turn, Dr. Edman often uttered exclamations of joy.

Edman's material for the weekend had included giving the guests a spiritual inventory to take. While we talked of sacred things, one of the inventory's questions kept coming back to me: "Is the Lord Jesus Christ real to me: a living, bright reality?" I knew Dr. Edman's answer would have been a resounding, "Yes!" I could see it in his face. He literally glowed with Christ's presence. He was a sensitive, godly man who knew what it was to walk with the King of kings in intimate fellowship.

Throughout the years since that retreat, I have often reflected on the summary of Dr. Edman's inventory because it revealed the secret of this man's closeness with God: "The Lord Jesus Christ Himself is the adequate answer to my every problem, perplexity, circumstance, opportunity."

I left the staff of The Firs with my wife and five children in September of 1967 to come to Texas to help start Pine Cove Conference Center. I came to Texas and Dr. Edman went to heaven. The account of Dr. Edman's finish is found in the dedication to an edition of his book *The Disciplines of Life*. I'd like to reprint it here:

In the Presence of the King

September 22, 1967, after nine months of being laid up with critical heart trouble, Dr. Edman stood in the chapel of Wheaton College and began his message to the student body with these words, "This will be the first time in more than ten months that I have attempted to speak in public. But I want you to consider with me an invitation to visit a King."

In the middle of the message he succumbed to a heart attack and entered into the presence of the King of kings and Lord of lords.

No man was more disciplined than Dr. Edman, and he often dwelt on discipline in his messages. He served as President of Wheaton College for 25 years (1940-1965), and 2 years as Chancellor. He was not only an educator, but was a missionary to the Quichua Indians in the Andes, Ecuador, South America, from 1923 to 1928. Dr. Edman was born in Chicago on May 9, 1900.[2]

Dr. Edman finished as he lived—thinking only of the King. What a fabulous end to a faithful race.

FINISHING STRONG

Calvin Miller quotes the wag who said, "I have seen the future; it is very much like the present, only longer."[3] Stretched out before you as you hit your senior years is an expanse of time to be filled selfishly or sacrificially. May we become what Martin Janis calls "seasoned citizens," not merely senior citizens.[4] May we creatively, effectively, vibrantly strive toward the goal of Christlikeness. May we, through the power and strength of the Lord Jesus Christ, make the last part the very best part.

I haven't finished the race yet, but I am definitely nearer than when I started this book. (So are you, by the way.) With the necessary losses of aging, I have finished some things, however. I've mentioned my arthritic hip a few times. Nothing has ever made me feel my own mortality more intensely than this bum joint, except perhaps the death of my dad. Some things are already finished for me. One of these happens to be my favorite leisure activity: running. I can't pursue it with the intensity I once did. I ain't no Bo Jackson, and marathons are history.

The week before hip surgery was scheduled, I spoke at our ministry's annual Colorado family camp. What a wonderful week it was—seeing old friends, meeting new ones, and sharing God's Word and wondrous creation. There could be no better place, I thought, to make my final run. For the last time I pulled on my windsuit and stretched out. The dawn had just broken; it was barely light when I set out from our lodge at Trail West toward Buena Vista, some six miles away. Each step was invigorating as the chill mountain air filled my lungs and cooled my sweat-soaked face. The deep, gnawing pain in my hip served as a constant reminder that this run would be the last run. The miles melted away in the joy of crossing mountain streams and seeing Mt. Princeton loom fourteen thousand feet above me.

When I neared the four-mile mark, I spied three figures in the hazy distance. I couldn't make out their faces until I drew much closer. What an enormous surprise to see Doug, Mike, and Joe, standing, waiting. With a big grin, Doug thrust a large glass of orange juice into my hand. "We're going to run the last part with you, Don." And they did. What an encouragement to wind things up with friends at my side. And that wasn't the half of it.

When we ran the final stretch into Buena Vista, there sat Sara, Doug's wife, at the wheel of a Suburban, doors flung wide open. From the vehicle's speakers loudly blared the recorded noise of a huge cheering crowd. I got a massive ovation as I crossed the final finish line, all thanks to some friends who went out of their way to care. The town of Buena Vista, Colorado, probably didn't think much of my welcome, but it sure made me feel good. Make that *great*. It was a tiny foretaste of heaven.

Now, even more than before, I want to finish well.

REFLECTIONS

1. Make it a habit now to find strength from the food of God's table.

2. Realize that God is waiting to be all you need Him to be right now.

3. Memorize these verses of Scripture: Isaiah 40:31; 2 Timothy 1:7; Philippians 4:13.

4. Recognize that being dependent does not destroy your dignity (Galatians 5:16).

CHAPTER 14

FINISH LIKE A PRO

I'm writing this final chapter from Little Cayman, the smallest of three islands in the Caribbean cluster. Access here is limited to either water or grass-covered runway. We came by the latter.

Twenty-five people inhabit Little Cayman, so Pearl and I have increased the population by nearly 10 percent. Bicycles carry us to church and to the store. It is a lovely, peaceful place.

Long-time friends and former marathoning buddies Doug and Sara Boyd have graciously offered the use of their condominium so I could complete this book without distraction. But there are distractions nonetheless—not the least of which is the glittering ocean front and white sandy beach. I decided to risk the new hip a little, pull on my running shoes, and walk and jog a few miles each morning. It is exhilarating, even though these days I'm more walk than jog.

Savoring the exhaustion, sweat pouring off my face, the satisfaction of short breaths—it all comes back to me. Why I loved running in the first place. Why I ran marathons.

I remember the Houston marathon as my best. Doug and Sara waited at the finish line, holding my warm-up suit. I placed my arms around their necks as they lifted my legs and eased them into my running suit and led me, totally spent, to the Gatorade tent.

Now, years later, I wonder if life isn't meant to be lived like that. We pound the pavement without surrender till we cross the line. The hot tub and Gatorade await, but they're available only after the race is done. The accoutrements of the finish feel and taste good *only if we have finished.* Everything stinks if we quit early. The trophies of triumph are placed in other hands.

I never ran a marathon to win the race. The breaking of the tape was for younger legs and fleeter feet. But I always ran to finish. That's the way God intended us to run the race of life. To let up and lie down is to miss the joy of the apostle Paul, who could write that he had "finished the course."

NOT FINISHING AIN'T FUN

Dallas's White Rock and California's Avenue of the Giants were two marathons I didn't finish. The temperature was high enough at both that I became dehydrated and was forced to quit at mile fourteen. I had even watched *Chariots of Fire* the night before. No good.

In the best of conditions, when I run, I sweat so much I look like a leaky radiator. When your radiator is empty, you overheat and blow an engine. That's what my body did in Dallas and California, the truth of Galatians 5:7 ringing in my ears: "You were running well." Standing and watching others finish and celebrate taught me some life lessons, notably this: It is far more fun to finish than it is to faint and fail and feel like a flop.

In life, many start out with a blast and finish a bust. I actually think there are more poor finishes than good ones, a phenomenon that may only increase as the Pepsi generation ages.

To illustrate the fact that few truly finish life well, Dr. Vernon Grounds carted a box full of biographies to the first session of our doctoral class some years ago. We students were allowed to select any of the biographies to read and report on to the class. The common denominator of all the books was that while they told the stories of great men used mightily by God, each man somehow blew it in the end. The list of reasons for failure was varied: sex, success, greed, marital problems, family difficulties, emotional burnout, addictive behaviors, poor interpersonal relationships. No matter how much God had used these men in the past, not one managed a solid finish. The reality was sobering.

The Bible is full of similar sobering reminders of folks who failed to finish well. We've mentioned many already in this book. Idolatry got Gideon. With Samson, it was sex. Eli was just plain lazy. Noah got drunk. Lot committed incest. Judas succumbed to greed. Why do so many fail?

FIZZLING BEFORE THE FINISH

As Vince Lombardi, late coach of the Green Bay Packers, said, "Fatigue makes cowards of us all." In my thirty-plus years of ministry, I have seen senior men and women grow weary toward the end. The finish line may be in view, yet some simply give up. They don't want to play the game of life anymore. They wait out the remainder of life benched with emotional injuries, viewing the rest of the contest in street clothes.

Some take themselves out of the game prematurely through the tragedy of suicide. They want to get it all over with and save their families the hassle and grief. A couple living next door to my parents made a pact; the husband shot his ailing wife and then himself. Ironically, their choices only caused their loved ones more heartache.

Other men and women sometimes slip quietly away from the struggle, leaving behind the problems, escaping to a new,

anonymous life somewhere else. They simply disappear, dis-
carding their former existence like a worn coat. You wonder if
they've gone into hiding in a federal witness protection program. Incredibly, a pastor I know did something very much like
this—deserting his family and life, only to surface months later
in another state.

Others who cannot cope drop out without actually leaving.
They retreat within the walls of their homes, refusing to participate in activities. Life overwhelms them, and frustrated by its
seeming futility and fearsome hurdles, they become like the living dead.

Louise always made Herb promise that she'd be the first to
go. When an aneurysm unexpectedly took his life, Louise was
left behind, angry, grief-stricken, and horribly alone. Her ther-
apist commented that she aged twenty years overnight. Ten
years later, feebled by arthritis and Parkinson's disease, she lives
with a daughter and son-in-law who care deeply but who cannot pierce the fog of self-pity surrounding her. She rarely goes
out, seldom answers the phone, scarcely speaks, and never
laughs. Never having rebounded from Herb's loss, she's chosen
to run from life rather than live it.

These are poor finishes. What tragedies when you consider
what might have been!

THE WAY OF THE WORLD IS TO CRASH AND BURN

The apostle Paul wrote of other poor finishes in Philippians
3:18-19, where he described the enemies of Christ as those
"whose god is their appetite, and whose glory is in their shame,
who set their minds on earthly things." Their finish will be
"destruction," wrote Paul.

Enemies of the cross of Christ crowd our culture today. Some are those who will not accept the simplicity of Jesus' sacrifice and make human performance a condition of salvation.

Other enemies, from Paul's description, are people who live without restraint. Their "god is their appetite." They indulge till they bulge. They live to eat...and to party and play. There is no Lord in their lives, only lust. No triumph, just toys. All world and no worship. They set their minds on the things down here, not what's up there. They glory in their shame, proudly singing with Sinatra, "I Did It My Way." With these words, reservations are made for a truly hot spot. Hell is a lousy finish. Nobody wants to go down in flames.

You can be a Christian and also live for the temporal instead of the eternal. We're not talking about a finish in hell here, but an unworthy end. A believer named Demas decided the allure of the world beat hanging around with a broke, near-sighted, jailbird apostle, so he deserted Paul for the sights and sounds of the big city, Thessalonica (2 Timothy 4:10). His name goes down in biblical history as one of the original Benedict Arnolds. Not the way you'd want to be remembered, is it?

The vast majority of folks in our world are enemies of the cross of Christ whether or not they know it. They are enemies when they deny its power. They are enemies when they live chiefly for the things of earth. Death is a tragedy if it means you will be leaving everything you have been living for.

There are risk factors involved in living for the here and now. Seniors whose god is literally their stomach are asking for trouble if they ignore principles of good nutrition and exercise. Setting our minds on earthly things won't enhance life, either.

Ray Ortlund quotes Hosea 7:9 as proof that being hung up on materialism and the things of the world ages us like nothing else: "Worshiping foreign gods has sapped their strength, but they don't know it. Ephraim's hair is turning gray, and he doesn't even realize how old and weak he is" (TLB). Comments Ortlund: "Listen, there's nothing that can age you like taking on the spirit of the world and mingling among the worriers, the jet set, the status seekers, the materialists, the fearful, the rat-racers, the competitors. There's nothing like these contacts to achieve that sagging posture and those old, bored eyes. Cousin What's-his-name will see you after a few months and he'll think, 'My, how he's aged.'"[1]

For Christians who engage in self-indulgent lifestyles, it is time to wake up before it's too late. "Let us behave properly," Paul wrote the Roman Christians, "...not in carousing and drunkenness, not in sexual promiscuity and sensuality, not in strife and jealousy. But put on the Lord Jesus Christ, and make no provision for the flesh in regard to its lusts" (Romans 13:13-14).

God's principle is clear: We are to go hard for Him till our earthly lives are over (Philippians 3:14). You can't make a good finish if you quit early. Determine now that you won't sink into senior adulthood as if it were an overstuffed easy chair and you a graying couch potato viewing the panorama of life on a big-screen TV.

The Lord warns the church of Philadelphia: "I am coming quickly; hold fast what you have, in order that no one take your crown" (Revelation 3:11). What a tragedy it is when one runs much of the race well only to fizzle and falter at the end (Galatians 5:7).

Most of the life of King Hezekiah in the Old Testament was characterized by reverence for God and a healthy, holy attitude toward the things of God. But Hezekiah fizzled at the finish. When it was announced that the end of his life was near, he begged God for an extension. God gave him fifteen years, but the final fifteen did not make for a fine finish. Hezekiah lost the temple treasury to the Babylonians and fathered a good-for-nothing son named Manasseh whose fifty-five-year reign denigrated all that his father had lived for (see Isaiah 39:1-8, 2 Kings 20).

I don't want to go out like that.

WHAT IT TAKES TO FINISH

We don't have to finish poorly. I've observed six characteristics common to men and women who finish strong. Most who finish rather than flop seem to possess each quality to some degree or another.

1. Good finishers are goal-oriented. Too many of us are like the guy who said, "Ready, fire, aim!" No wonder we get disoriented in our senior years. We aren't focusing on the goal of a strong finish and all that it entails. We aren't focusing on anything except perhaps reaching retirement! To go back to our race analogy, moving up the finish line a few miles so you have time to celebrate down here isn't fair. Running a half-marathon won't cut it, either. Life is to be run flat out to the finish. Even if you've already quit early, it's not too late to get going again and rejoin the race!

Life is to be purposeful right up to the end—the celebration victories are for heaven, not here and now. You don't want to be heading for the end zone only to have the ball knocked from your hand before you cross the goal line, do you? (Ask much-maligned Dallas Cowboy Leon Lett, who trotted blissfully toward the end zone in Super Bowl XXII only to have Buffalo Bill Don Beebe rip the football from him at the last second. It's no fun to be remembered as the guy who partied early and failed to score.)

According to radio talk show host Rush Limbaugh, Steve Sable of NFL Films gave this instruction to the cameramen in charge of covering Super Bowl XXIII: "FLAP—Finish Like a Pro." Sable's directions were simple: keep filming, stay on your man, don't quit or the camera might miss something crucial. Finish like a pro, the professional that you are. That's good advice for TV…and great advice for life!

2. Good finishers have a network of accountability. Behavior that is observed always improves. When you have a group of friends looking over your shoulder, asking the tough questions with love, holding you accountable for your actions, attitudes, and walk with the Lord, you will likely finish well.

King Saul had the opportunity to let the prophet Samuel hold him accountable. But Saul never allowed himself to be vulnerable and transparent before Samuel. Instead he tried to cover up and rationalize sin (1 Samuel 15:12-22). Unlike David, who made himself accountable to Jonathan, Samuel, and, later, Nathan, Saul refused to let others in. His tragic end as a suicide on the field of battle speaks volumes about the trouble of keeping yourself aloof from wise, concerned counsel.

Each of us needs people—our spouse, friends, business associates—to whom we can be accountable. If what we are doing passes their scrutiny, we are probably on track.

3. Good finishers are disciplined. Discipline means I do what I have to do rather than what I want to do. Discipline involves the physical, emotional, spiritual, and intellectual parts of our being. Human nature wants to take the easy way out. To this we have to say no! "I treat my body roughly and make it serve me" (1 Corinthians 9:27 author's translation).

Physically, discipline involves eating right and exercising. Emotionally, discipline means dealing with our lack of forgiveness so we can be free to love and to give generously of ourselves to others. Spiritually, it's out of the bed and into the Book, developing intimacy with our precious Savior. Intellectually, we keep exercising our minds by learning, reading, experimenting, observing. We expand our horizons by trying new things and developing projects designed to stretch us.

When you know something is right and you pay the price by doing it, then comes the joy. Could that be part of what Jesus had in mind when He said, "If anyone wishes to come after Me, let him deny himself, and take up his cross daily, and follow Me" (Luke 9:23)? It was for the "joy set before Him" that Jesus "endured the cross" (Hebrews 12:2). Obedience to God results in genuine joy.

4. Good finishers are developing an ever deeper intimacy with God. This means making time daily to feed upon God's Word, memorizing and meditating upon it. It means taking time to pray, and time to be still and know that He is God. With many folks, these spiritual disciplines only seem to manifest themselves in periods of crisis. It may seem easier to call upon God in a fourth and long situation than in a first and ten. When you feel shredded by the Cuisinart of life, you know it's impossible to go it alone...but the truth is you need Him always. Daily time with Him lays the groundwork for a good finish. "Blessed is the man who listens to me, watching daily at my doors, waiting at my doorway" (Proverbs 8:34 NIV).

5. *Good finishers are always looking forward.* Looking forward means getting excited about what is ahead. It means never losing the thrill of tomorrow. Every day seems a bit like Christmas. God designed it that way!

Looking forward also means forgetting how we've blown it in the past and pressing on to the fabulous future (Philippians 3:13-14). It's never too late to get serious and get going with God. Samuel encouraged the nation Israel, "Do not be afraid, you've done all this evil; yet do not turn away from the Lord, but serve the Lord with all your heart" (1 Samuel 12:20 NIV). Israel never really took him up on the advice, but you can. "'For I know the plans I have for you,' declares the Lord, 'plans to prosper you and not to harm you, plans to give you hope and a future'" (Jeremiah 29:11 NIV).

6. *Good finishers may let up, but they don't give up.* As you near the finish line, you may find you are not able to do as much as you used to do. But you can still do something.

Since my running days are pretty much over, I've done a lot of biking, occasionally putting the foot to the pedal and tackling one of our state's many races. The city of Tyler, Texas, sponsors the Beauty and the Beast bicycle race each spring, and I've done the twenty-five-, fifty-, and sixty-mile segments through the years. (I haven't been ambitious enough to shoot for the hundred. Yet. So far when the urge comes upon me, I lie down till it goes away.)

The Beauty and the Beast route winds its way through some of the most gorgeous pine-laden roads in the state—and also over some of the toughest hills. The race is called the "Beauty" because of the azaleas and dogwood which decorate the countryside…and the "Beast" because of the biggest hill of all just a few miles from the finish line. The Beast is to Tyler what Heartbreak Hill is to the Boston Marathon. A mega-hill. A bone crusher. A killer.

Last year my younger friend Mike and I signed up for the fifty-mile ride. The Beast was an optional part of the course. We came to the forty-mile marker and were faced with a choice. Do we tackle the Beast, or do we choose to take the remaining ten miles back to town on a gradual incline and flat surface? As far as I was concerned, my body was telling me the decision had already been made, but I turned to Mike and let him choose since this was his first race. I think the agony he saw in my face was enough to make him have mercy upon me, and we took the easy way home.

And that was okay. At least we stayed in the race.

My friend Bobby Wolff says he has so many things wrong with him that he can no longer golf and fish, but he can still go to the club and drink coffee with the "trash" (his affectionate name for his buddies). He sums up his troubles with a laugh: "There are so many things wrong with me that I can take just about any pill and it's bound to work somewhere."

You let up, but you don't give up. And you keep a sense of humor through it all.

DO IT NOW!

Our precious friends Tom and Olive Mandrell have been mentioned quite a bit throughout this book. Their names purposely have not been disguised. You see, it was with Tom and

Olive in mind that I began this project. Of the many fine examples of godly seniors, this vibrant couple stood out in my mind as models to follow.

Close? You bet. Olive's eyes were literally Tom's eyes much of the time. Tom, a pilot during World War II, was severely burned when his plane was shot down over Germany. A British doctor performed a skin graft without anesthetic. Stateside doctors said they couldn't have done it better. However, as a result of all the trauma one of Tom's physical problems—calcification of the spine—was aggravated.

Tom emerged from the war unable to turn his head from side to side. From then on, whenever he drove the car, Olive functioned as his eyes at intersections and turns. She warned him of oncoming traffic, telling him when it was safe to proceed. They worked together so smoothly that all signals were usually relayed without causing so much as a break in the conversation.

During Tom's lengthy career with Dow Chemical, the Mandrells lived all over the world. At retirement they continued the travel trend—educating themselves about a culture or studying an avocation, then visiting the country or plunging into hands-on activity. Always learning and growing, Tom and Olive thrived on tackling new experiences whether it was snorkeling, cross-country skiing, Japanese fish rubbing, photography, or personal computing. You name it, they tried it or it was on their schedule of future events.

Meticulously Tom and Olive planned their retirement, deciding long before it was time to retire where they would live and how they would live. They achieved a rare life balance between leisure and work. They found more than enough time for travel and recreation, family, church and Christian endeavors, and community involvement. Generously they included a "prophet's chamber" in their retirement home where visiting missionaries and speakers like this old itinerant preacher were always welcome.

Their home served as my base of operations whenever the Lord provided opportunities for me to minister in Austin. Even when I was in town and couldn't stay with them, Olive would whip up one of her world-class gourmet feasts and schedule me for supper. You couldn't say no, and you sure didn't want to anyway.

I looked forward to giving Tom and Olive an advance copy of this book. I knew they'd be embarrassed by the frequent mentions but wanted to tell them how much their example, like so many others, had meant to Pearl and me.

Now I'll never get the chance.

Not with Olive at least. You see, a few weeks after I started this chapter on Little Cayman, the phone call came to our offices with the news that Olive had suddenly finished like a pro. Tom and she had spent a few weeks mud fishing on the Texas coast with their entire family—kids, grandkids, siblings, in-laws. We saw them in Austin on December 19 and 26, when they made special trips to the church where I was the guest speaker. The next Sunday morning, January 2, Olive collapsed, never to reawaken.

"I feel like a one-armed paper hanger. It's been forty-eight years of an awful lot of precious memories," said Tom. Yes, it had. I don't want to think of this world without Olive...except for the fact I know she's in the next one in the presence of her heavenly Father waiting for us all.

Olive's passing leaves me with a sense of urgency which cuts through the fluff and funny stuff to expose raw nerve. I don't want to mince words with you. May the unexpected graduation of this precious lady shout it louder than I ever could: You might not be here tomorrow! Get it done today!

Like Paul, we can be sure of this very thing: "He who began a good work in us will perfect it until the day of Christ Jesus" (Philippians 1:6). Dr. V. Raymond Edman, who ran his race until the moment he was called home, said it well:

After years of observation one is ready to say that most of the people one has seen quit have quit too soon. Another week; a few more good licks; standing by just a little longer—and the whole situation would have opened into a larger phase. But, no! They were more practiced in quitting than in staying. Only recently one saw a man quit in spite of earnest counsel because he couldn't get what he wanted; two days later the very thing he wanted came looking for him, and he wasn't there. He had quit too soon. It is always too soon to quit.[2]

You really do want to finish like a pro, don't you? It's not too late for any of us.

My prayer for you and me as we mature is that the vision and passion for a strong finish will intensify, and that absolutely nothing will stop us from doing it up right. Press on, persevere, and point toward home. Oh to be able to shout with the Savior, "Tetelestai!—It is finished!" so that the watching throng knows we gave it our best shot.

REFLECTIONS:

1. Have you given God you body (Romans 12:1-2), your blessings (Hebrews 13:15), and your belongings (Philippians 4:18)?

2. Have you established relationships of accountability with other believers? There's nothing like a brother or sister in Christ to hold you responsible for your actions and keep you on the right track so you can finish well.

NOTES

CHAPTER ONE: HOW OLD IS OLD...AND WHAT'S IT TO YOU?

1. INFOsearch 3.0 (Arlington, Texas: The Computer Assistant, copyright Humor Data by Broadman, 1990): 1360.

2. Thomas K. Tewell, "The Art of Aging Gracefully," sermon printed in *An Invitation to Graceful Living* (Houston: Memorial Drive Presbyterian Church, Oct. 18, 1992).

3. Auren Uris, Over 50: *The Definitive Guide to Retirement* (Radnor, Pa.: Chilton, 1979), 11.

4. Frank Minirth, John Reed, and Paul Meier, *Beating the Clock: A Guide to Maturing Successfully* (Grand Rapids: Baker, 1985), 13.

5. J. William Mason and Lillian Mason, *You Can Be Happy Though Retired* (Dallas: Crescendo, 1975), 107.

6. Paul Faulkner, *Making Things Right When Things Go Wrong: Ten Proven Ways to Put Your Life in Order* (Ft. Worth, Texas: Sweet, 1986), 83.

7. Jerry M. Stubblefield, *A Church Ministering to Adults* (Nashville, Tenn.: Broadman, 1986), 91.

8. Leland Frederick Cooley and Lee Morrison Cooley, *How to Avoid the Retirement Trap* (Los Angeles: Nash, 1972), 28.

9. Martin A. Janis, *The Joys of Aging* (Dallas: Word, 1988), 33.

10. Melinda Beck, "The Geezer Boom," *Newsweek* 114, no. 27, sp. ed. (Winter/Spring 1990): 62.

11. Minirth, Reed, and Meier, 13.

12. Edmund Fuller, ed., *12,500 Anecdotes for All Occasions* (New York: Avenel, 1970), 119.

13. Dale Evans Rogers and Floyd Thatcher, *The Home Stretch* (Waco, Texas: Word, 1986), 86.

14. Chuck Yeager, *Yeager: An Autobiography* (New York, Bantam, 1985), 421-22.

15. Stephen Westmoreland, "My Assignment?" *Self-Help-Newsletter of Discovery* (May 3, 1989): 3.

16. Charles Colson and Ellen Santilli Vaughn, *Against the Night: Living in the New Dark Ages* (Ann Arbor, Mich.: Servant Publications, 1989), 56.

17. American Association of Boomers, Pamphlet: "Boomers Come of Age," (Irving, Texas: American Association of Boomers, n.d.), 2.

CHAPTER TWO: RETIREMENT: THE THREE P'S

1. Horace L. Kerr, *Coming of Age: Senior Adults and the Churches* (Nashville: Convention, 1986), 11.
2. Beck, 68.
3. Adapted in *My Generation* (September/October 1992) American Association of Boomers, 3, from A. Haeworth Robertson's *What Every Taxpayer Should Know* (Washington, D.C.: Retirement Policy Institute, 1992).
4. Karen Meredith, "Social Security: Trust Fund or IOU?" *My Generation* (January/February 1992): 4.
5. B. F. Skinner and M. E. Vaughan, *Enjoy Old Age: A Program of Self-Management* (New York: Warner, 1983), 77.
6. Paul Fremont Brown, *From Here to Retirement: Planning Now for the Rest of Your Life* (Waco, Texas: Word, 1988), 84.
7. Skinner and Vaughan, 77.
8. Beck, 63,68.
9. Meredith, 4.
10. Beck, 62-68.
11. Nancy Gibbs and Richard N. Ostling, "God's Billy Pulpit," *Time* 142, no. 20 (November 15, 1993): 70.
12. Daniel J. Levinson, *The Seasons of a Man's Life* (New York: Ballantine, 1978), 49.
13. Uris, 12.
14. Uris, 149.
15. Skinner and Vaughan, 88.
16. American Association of Retired Persons, *How to Plan Your Successful Retirement: Looking Ahead,* rev. ed. (Glenview, Tenn.: Scott, Foresman, and Co., Lifelong Learning Division, 1988), 5.
17. John Piper, *Desiring God: Meditations of a Christian Hedonist* (Portland, Ore.: Multnomah, 1986), 186.

CHAPTER THREE: WHEN IN DOUBT, READ THE DIRECTIONS

1. Stubblefield, 96-97.
2. Stubblefield, 96-97.

3. Stubblefield, 97.
4. Paul Tournier, *Learn to Grow Old* (New York: Harper and Row, 1972), 123.
5. Alfred, Lord Tennyson, "Ulysses," *Tennyson's Poetry: Authoritative Texts, Juvenalia and Early Responses, Criticism,* Robert W. Hill, Jr., comp. and ed., Norton Critical ed. (New York: W. W. Norton, 1971), 53-54.
6. A. Boyd Luter, Jr., "Philippians," *Evangelical Commentary on the Bible,* ed. Walter A. Elwell (Grand Rapids, Mich.: Baker, 1989), 1034-48.
7. Gail MacDonald, *A Step Farther and Higher* (Sisters, Ore.: Questar, 1993), 5.
8. C. G. "Spike" and Darnell White, *I Need You: Being Friends with Your Grandkids* (Sisters, Ore.: Questar, 1989), 37.

CHAPTER FOUR: THE FRIENDS AND FAMILY NETWORK
1. Helen Gurley Brown, *The Late Show* (New York: William Morrow, 1993), 51-52.
2. Minirth, Reed, and Meier, 40.
3. Janis, 77.
4. Henri J. M. Nouwen, *In the Name of Jesus: Reflections on Christian Leadership* (New York: Crossroad, 1991), 59-60.
5. Bill Cosby, *Time Flies* (New York: Doubleday, 1987), 173.
6. Tournier, 94.
7. Gurley Brown, 41.
8. Judith Viorst, *Necessary Losses* (Austin, Texas: S and S, 1986), 204.
9. Tim Stafford, *As Our Years Increase: Loving, Caring, Preparing: A Guide* (Grand Rapids, Zondervan, 1989), 48.

CHAPTER FIVE: WHOSE LIFE IS IT ANYWAY?
1. Barbara Deane, *Getting Ready for a Great Retirement* (Colorado Springs: NavPress, 1992), 17.
2. Deane, 140.
3. Paul Rees, *The Adequate Man: Paul in Philippians* (Westwood, N. J.: Revell, 1959), 27.
4. Mason and Mason, 33-34.
5. Vernon C. Grounds, "Liberating Loss," in *Our Daily Bread,* 37, no. 8, November 5, 1993).

CHAPTER SIX: STAYING STABLE IN THE STORM

1. Erma Bombeck, *A Marriage Made in Heaven...Or Too Tired for an Affair* (New York: HarperCollins, 1993), 244.
2. Stephen Sapp, *Full of Years: Aging and the Elderly in the Bible and Today* (Nashville: Abingdon, 1987), 140.
3. Sapp, 158.
4. Sapp, 140-41.
5. Paul Brand and Phillip Yancey, *Pain: The Gift Nobody Wants* (New York: HarperCollins, 1993), 285.
6. Charles Jones, *Life Is Tremendous* (Wheaton, Ill.: Tyndale House, 1968), 46.
7. Peter F. Gunther, comp., *A Frank Boreham Treasury* (Chicago: Moody, 1984), 97-104.
8. John Mackinnon, unpublished letter to the church at 1100 Washington, Waco, Texas.

CHAPTER SEVEN: PLANNING FOR GRADUATION

1. Wallace McRae, "Reincarnation," in *Cowboy Curmudgeon* (Layton, Utah: Gibbs Smith, 1992). All rights reserved. Used by permission.
2. Minirth, Reed, and Meier, 30-31.
3. Charles Sell, *Transitions: The Stages of Adult Life* (Chicago: Moody Press, 1985), 219.
4. Lloyd Cory, *Quotable Quotations* (Wheaton, Ill.: Victor, 1985), 18.
5. Ann Landers, printed in the *Tyler Morning Telegraph,* November 15, 1993.
6. Katie Letcher Lyle, "A Gentle Way to Die," *Newsweek,* (March 2, 1992): 14.
7. J. Kerby Anderson, *Living Ethically in the 90's* (Wheaton, Ill.: Victor Books, 1990), 199.
8. Joni Eareckson Tada, *When Is It Right to Die?* (Grand Rapids: Zondervan, 1992), 58-60.
9. Tada, 60.
10. William P. Barker, *A Savior for All Seasons* (Old Tappan, N. J.: Revell, 1986), 191.
11. Irene O'Brien, "Life Is for the Living," article printed in the Federated Church bulletin, Columbus, Neb., July 11, 1993.

CHAPTER EIGHT: THE MIND OF CHRIST

1. Paul B. Maves, *Faith for the Older Years: Making the Most of Life's Second Half* (Minneapolis: Augsburg, 1986), 58.
2. Keith L. Brooks, "Philippians: the Epistle of Christian Joy," from *Teach Yourself the Bible* (Chicago: Moody Bible Institute, 1963), 17.
3. Tournier, 142.
4. AARP, 46.
5. Jerry White, *Choosing Plan A in a Plan B World: Living Out the Lordship of Christ* (Colorado Springs: NavPress, 1987), 149.
6. Gerald F. Hawthorne, *Philippians,* vol. 43, *Word Biblical Commentary,* David A. Hubbard, Glenn W. Barker, John D. W. Watts, and Ralph P. Martin, eds. (Waco, Texas: Word, 1983), 121.
7. Hawthorne, 120.
8. Sell, 243.
9. Jimmy Carter and Rosalynn Carter, *Everything to Gain: Making the Most of the Rest of Your Life* (New York: Random House, 1987), 95.
10. Deane, 36.
11. Deane, 37.
12. Janis, 83.
13. Janis, 147.
14. Leland Ryken, *Leisure in Christian Perspective* (Portland, Ore.: Multnomah, 1987), 231.
15. Harold Clinebell, *Basic Types of Pastoral Care and Counseling: Resources for the Ministry of Healing and Growth* (Nashville: Abingdon, 1984), 209.

CHAPTER NINE: DEEPENING THE RELATIONSHIP

1. Gurley Brown, 38.
2. Gurley Brown, 13.
3. J. B. Lightfoot, *Saint Paul's Epistle to the Philippians: A Revised Text with Introduction, Notes and Dissertations,* reprint (Grand Rapids: Zondervan, 1913), 144.
4. Maves, 24.
5. Stafford, 102.
6. Stafford, 103.

7. Dwight Eisenhower, in *Quotable Quotations*, Lloyd Cory, comp. (Wheaton, Ill.: Victor, 1985), 142.
8. Colena M. Anderson, *Don't Put on Your Slippers Yet* (Grand Rapids, Mich.: Zondervan, 1971), 33.
9. Bruce, 96.
10. Brown, 103.

CHAPTER TEN: EVIDENCE THAT THE KING IS IN RESIDENCE

1. "World Overlooks Death of Recluse for Four Years," *Tyler Morning Telegraph*, vol. 62, no. 718 (Wednesday, October 27, 1993), Section 1, p. 1, col. 6.
2. Piper, 19.
3. C. S. Lewis, "The Weight of Glory," *The Weight of Glory and Other Essays*, 1965, quoted in Piper, 77-78.
4. Piper, 77-78.
5. F. F. Bruce, Philippians: A Good News Commentary (San Francisco: Harper and Row, 1983), 116.
6. Kerr, 18.
7. Kerr, 18.
8. Tim Hansel, *You Gotta Keep on Dancin'* (Elgin, Ill.: Chariot Family Publishing, 1985), 54.

CHAPTER ELEVEN: ON YOUR KNEES

1. From *Construction Digest*, quoted in *Quotable Quotations*, Cory, comp., 297.
2. Henry G. Bosch, "How to Retire," in *Our Daily Bread*, 34, no. 12, March 21, 1990.
3. Ruth Harms Calkin, "The Reason," from *Lord, I Keep Running Back to You* by Ruth Harms Calkin. Published by Tyndale House Publishers, Inc., © 1979. Used by permission. All rights reserved.
4. Hawthorne, 184.
5. Bombeck, 206.
6. Barbara Johnson, *Fresh Elastic for Stretched out Moms* (Grand Rapids: Revell, 1986), 24.
7. W. Bingham Hunter, *The God Who Hears* (Downers Grove, Ill.: InterVarsity Press, 1986), 135.

8. Joseph Aldrich, *Prayer Summits* (Portland, Ore.: Multnomah, 1992), 183-84.

9. Sammy Tippit with Jerry Jenkins, *No Matter What the Cost: An Autobiography* (Nashville: Thomas Nelson, 1993), 255.

CHAPTER TWELVE: A WISE INVESTMENT

1. Unknown.
2. AARP, 5.
3. Denise M. Topolnicki, "Beat the Five Threats to Your Retirement," *Money* 22:11 (November 1993): 70.
4. Topolnicki, 70.
5. Topolnicki, 71.
6. Topolnicki, 72.
7. Topolnicki, 73.
8. Auren Uris, 109.
9. Elizabeth Greene, Stephen G. Greene, and Jennifer Moo Generation Prepares to Transfer Its Trillions," *The Chronicle of Philanthropy*, VI, no. 3 (November 16, 1993): 1.
10. Ann Landers, printed in the *Tyler Morning Telegraph*, January 29, 1994.

CHAPTER THIRTEEN: LEARNING TO LEAN

1. Annie Johnson Flint, "He Giveth More Grace," *The New Church Hymnal* (n.p.: Lexicon Music, Inc., 1976), 33.
2. V. Raymond Edman, *The Disciplines of Life*, Crusade ed. (Minneapolis: World Wide, 1948), 5.
3. Calvin Miller, *Becoming: Your Self in the Making* (Old Tappan, N. J.: Revell, 1987), 104.
4. Janis, 163.

CHAPTER FOURTEEN: FINISH LIKE A PRO

1. Ray Ortlund and Anne Ortlund, *The Best Half of Life* (Glendale, Calif.: Gospel Light, 1976), 33.
2. Edman, 140.

ABOUT THE AUTHOR

Popular pastor, teacher, and speaker Don Anderson tours the Southwest giving Bible classes and seminars during the fall, winter, and spring months. During the spring and summer, Don Anderson Ministries sponsors conferences and youth and family camps. Don also speaks at Bible conferences in various locations throughout the United States and Canada. His audiences of business and professional men and women, homemakers, and tradespeople, testify that his refreshing teaching makes the Scriptures "come alive" for them.

Don Anderson graduated from Northwestern College in 1955 with a bachelor of arts, received a masters of theology from Dallas Theological Seminary in 1959, and earned a doctorate of ministry from Talbot School of Theology in 1990. Don has been in Christian ministry for more than thirty years, serving as a Young Life staff member, youth pastor, program director at The Firs Bible and Missionary Conference, executive director of Pine Cove Conference Center, and pastor of Hide-A-Way Lake and Emerald Bay community churches. Since 1972 he has directed the non-profit organization, Don Anderson Ministries, headquartered in Tyler, Texas. Devoted to excellence in Christian camping, counseling, and communications, the Ministries is funded by private donations, is overseen by an independent board of directors, and is a charter member of the Evangelical Council for Financial Accountability.

Don Anderson has many audio and video cassette tapes based on his teachings that are produced by the Ministries. A quarterly magazine, *The Grapevine,* is distributed to some ten thousand homes. If you would like to receive information about the materials, classes, camps, and conferences offered by the Ministries, please contact us at the following:

Don Anderson Ministries

P. O. Box 6611
Tyler, Texas 75711
903/597-3018
FAX 903/595-0678